IØ172716

Spectral Realms

No. 10 ‡ Winter 2019

Edited by S. T. Joshi

The spectral realms that thou canst see
With eyes veil'd from the world and me.

H. P. LOVECRAFT, "To a Dreamer"

SPECTRAL REALMS is published twice a year by Hippocampus Press,
P.O. Box 641, New York, NY 10156 (www.hippocampuspress.com).
Copyright © 2019 by Hippocampus Press.
All works are copyright © 2019 by their respective authors.
"Chiron's Burden—Pleiades Children" © 2019 by Kim Bo Yung.
Cover design by Daniel V. Sauer.
Hippocampus Press logo by Anastasia Damianakos.

ISBN 978-1-61498-236-4   ISSN 2333-4215

Contents

Poems

The Name on the Grave

Thomas Tyrrell

I sought a name to work into a tale
Among the ancient and forgotten dead.
Moving from grave to mossy grave I read
The names of those long gone to bliss or bale:
Fine sonorous southern names, but all would fail
To suit the story dreaming in my head,
Till shunned and set apart, as if in dread
I found a tombstone marked "Gamela Grayle."

The dreaming story woke within me then;
The world around me faded into dream.
Nothing existed for me but this theme
Until my tale was written down. But when
I read it through once more, it made me scream,
To guess what muse or demon held the pen.

Eurynomos

Wade German

At Delphi, there is a painting of Hades by Polygnotos. Depicted therein is Eurynomos. The Delphian guides say he is one of the spirits of the Underworld, who devours the flesh of corpses, leaving only their bones . . . He is of a blue-black colour, like that of meat flies, and he is shown with bared teeth and is seated upon a vulture's skin.–PAUSANIAS, *Description of Greece*

The meat-flies serve me with their million eyes;
Through them I see another over there,
Lying alone, all wrapped in cerement cloth.
This one is clean as she could ever be;
I'll drop her fleshless carcass and move on,
Crawling across the hill to get me more.
I'm always ravenous, so it is good
That Hades is replenished frequently.
Here it is, well hidden among the stones;
I must have passed him many times before.
A recent entry, this one; not yet ripe,
His putrefaction just a faint perfume,
And still a little subtle for my taste.
Perhaps I'll leave him yet; let him mature
Into a fly-blown thing, softer to chew,
A fruit more ripe for peeling sweeter flesh,
Flowering in his pestilential fumes
As all his seeping pus and ichor pools.
His sunken features, appositely pale,

Are oddly mottled yellow-red and black;
He must have been a victim of disease.
The Nosoi must be busy spreading plague;
I've seen a few just like this recently.
Now, as I see no other corpses near,
I'll settle down and chew his fat a while.
While not full-rotten yet, he comes prepared,
Well seasoned with the bitterest of herbs:
I taste a little insolence and pride;
He's savoury with malice, and there's spite.
His juices would suggest a jealous heart . . .
Undone by envy, this one, I suppose.
How strong his flavours flow, delicious in death!
I'm nearly done with this one.
                                    In the end,
They all corrupt with foulness, every one
But some grow even fouler on this side.
I've eaten bodies hidden very well,
But shown to me by their own spectral selves.
They are the ones old Charon has refused
A passage on his boat across the Styx
For they've received no funerary rites.
A burial is sacred, and completes
The final custom gods on men imposed,
And Hades will not have them incomplete.

Unlucky shades like those have sought me out
Across the quiet plain of skyless gloom,
Leaving a while their brethren spectral throngs
That wander on the darkling river shore,
Sharing a ban upon forgetfulness
That flows beyond, in realms forbidden them.
They come to me in very clever thought,
Thinking to bury proof of evidence—
To make their blameless bodies disappear
In hope of getting on the boatman's barge.
Asking me to remove it from all sight,
They lead me to their silent, ghosted house—
And bid me with all haste inherit it!
I devour their corpse; they go their way,
Thanking me in profusion. I then turn
To call a vulture for my messenger,
Who flies across the vaulted dome of night
To croak intelligence in Charon's ear.
For that is our agreement: deeds done cheap
Against the self to get oneself to Hell
Are impious, screaming for some punishment.
But there is hope.
                            Not all are so corrupt
As all these corpses that I must to eat;
My devotees are promising, in ways.

Once, when the mortals knew not of my name,
A man descended to the underworld
To fetch his bride from out the house of death.
Upon his useless voyage to us here
(When otherworldly music filled the halls
Of Hades, haunting it with eldritch art)
He learned my name by whispers from the dead,
And later uttered it upon the earth.
It took a tiny root; my cult was sown,
And blossomed frightfully, a thing obscure.
Their lot is numbered by a very few:
All outcast men and women, lowly ones
Who live like worms in tunnels of the earth.
They honour me by imitative means,
Performing what could be my holy rite:
Robbing the graves and newly risen tombs
Of liars, blasphemers—and criminals
Convicted by an honest, lawful curse
Some righteous victim once invoked by right.
My devotees go seeking only those:
Gnawing the putrid flesh from off their bones
And lapping liquefaction in the grave.
With foetid morsels filling up their mouths,
They leave behind them yawning, emptied tombs.
I've seen a spectre tremble in despair,

Sensing the things committed on its corpse . . .
So much the better, if it's swifter work,
When carrion overflows all Hell in heaps.
Ungrateful spirit I, if not to share—
They pick some unclean bones from off my plate.

Winter

Charles D. O'Connor III

Fall opens its somber eyes, and the summer skies turn leaden gray. Then the winds chill, whining and moaning, chanting funeral dirges across the land, lamenting the arrival of death's icy hand. But every animate being who dwells on the brink of consciousness must allow the fiery, painful cold to bless their vessel; dragging it through to the end—that last oblivious cycle of the seasons.

Every year in Andersonville the grassy fields realize this. The flowers drain themselves of color; wither and blacken, bowing; obeying winter's deadly touch on their fragile petals. Grass dries and rots, trees shed leaves that fall onto the grass in cascades. A man whose face evokes winter and graveyards gazes at the leaves falling, and a tear rolls down his face as he recalls memories of his children rushing through the grass and of his wife, who once loved to laugh and dance and smile; now lying below this sod; her formerly warm body now as cold as the wind, her timeless beauty wilting like the flowers, her supple skin drying like the grass, and her lithe body becoming withered like the trees.

He racks his brain this season remembering all the children who lived and loved and laughed and had fun during the spring and summer, as did his wife. These leaves are his fondest memories; now lying brown and decaying on the ground. He's old and can only remember and see his loved ones through the leaves. Each year his memories get worse to bear. Can he really rake the fields again and say goodbye to his memories once more? Now he rakes the leaves and the sun sets golden behind the bare, skeletal trees. Nothing remains except his rake as time and its mysteries sweep past him in the wind—it carries him away, erases him. Now everything that once lived is silent, the wind alone is left whining, moaning, and the field is clean of all leaves.

Conjuring in Cupid's Garden

Claire Smith

We'd set ourselves in a hammock
Between the trees amongst a sun-soaked grove.
We are sisters in sharing our laughter,
Share secrets and gossip about the neighbourhood
Share gossip about our neighbourhood.

One such time a boy approached;
We giggled, awkward at the sight.
A poor sailor boy with expectations
Proposed to us both with his salutations,
Proposed marriage to us with salutations.

His stupidity amused us, naïveté seemed to play
The strings of this unfortunate boy's heart.
We weren't going to give in to him an inch,
Relinquish to him a bit of our maidenhoods,
Relinquish to him gifts of our virginities.

My sister crossed fingers behind her back,
Swore she would keep a laurel about her neck;
She would become a sister of the church.
I watched his face fall in disappointment,
Watched his face drop due to our sanctity.

Then he turned his attentions onto my face;
I saw his demeanour appeal for me to comply,

Saw a desperate boy, intent on losing himself in me—
I wasn't going to give any of my love so easily,
Wouldn't give him my love so readily.

So in Cupid's garden this boy did despair
Along with so many of his comrades and kin.
We'd only spare them a lock of brown curled hair,
For nothing is as it seems—for this is Cupid's garden,
We are not the innocents Cupid's garden makes us seem—

We Witches summon
         Visions of young girls in Cupid's garden;
We Witches disguised
          Girls sitting in a hammock among the trees;
We Witches conjure
         Perfect magic tricks of beauty for a tease.

The Haunting Bones

Adam Bolivar

Two sisters by a river strolled
    The winding River Tay,
Beneath which dwells a beast of old,
    Or so the legends say.

The dark one pushed the fair one in:
    It was a jealous rage
That led her to commit this sin
    And nothing could assuage,

For handsome Jack the fair one loved,
    And she would marry him,
And so the dark one swiftly shoved
    Her sister on a whim.

The poor girl sank into the murk,
    Which gratified the beast
Who underneath was said to lurk
    And hunger for a feast.

When came the spring a minstrel found
    Upon the bank her bones
To craft a harp which had a sound
    Quite haunting in its tones.

Invited to a wedding feast
    The balladeer then was,

An irony which pleased the beast
 Who was this mischief's cause.

The sister who had hair of black,
 And was a murderess,
Was marrying now handsome Jack
 And wore a silken dress.

The balladeer the bone-harp played,
 Æthereal the sound;
A ghost in tatters all arrayed
 Bewailed: the girl who drowned—

"I once was Elspeth, fair of tress,
 Betrothed this day to wed;
I ought to wear that silken dress—
 Alas, but I am dead,

"For Eleanor my sister killed
 Me out of lust for Jack;
My heart beneath the Tay was stilled,
 For hers was cold and black."

Then Eleanor fled from the hall
 And nevermore was heard;
And ever would that harp enthrall
 When were the bones bestirred.

The Island

Christina Sng

So there they are,
The twin boats
That brought us
To this end,

Perched by the shore
To forever watch
The beatific sun rise
And fall with the tides,

While our bodies
Decompose in solitude
By the wilting coconut trees,
Surely resentful of our presence

But grateful when we finally
Break down and give them
A rush of nutrients to flower
Some fat coconuts for the monkeys.

Perhaps only then am I
Willing to leave, knowing
My life will be of some use
To the universe.

I do not move
My broken shattered body
But turn my eyes
To the stars,

Enjoying a moment
Of quiet serenity
Before the wretched
Monkeys take them.

The Promise of Eternity

Kurt Newton

A body, a tree,
carved with runic symbols,
letters cut to indignify
a heinous crime with mystery.

The man, a priest,
black robe rustling in the wind,
crows perched on gnarled branches
voicing their objection to the interruption of their feast.

With Bible gripped in rigor-mortised hand,
the holy man was taken down,
arcane symbols jutting from his brow
in a hideous bas-relief.

The tree, a sprawling oak,
used for Sunday family picnics
or a meeting-place for lovers under moonlit gaze,
possessed a darker, much more sinister history.

A hanging tree, in less enlightened days,
when man presumed command of evil
and yet evil had the upper hand,
when poor folk and knotted rope were on display for all to see.

A familiar landmark, a respected figure,
both connected by this unholy act of desecration,
perpetrated by a person or persons rooted
in the rolling landscape of the surrounding community.

But the Inspector Chief and his deputy
determined cause of death a suicide,
the ancient symbols self-inflicted, a troubled man,
a lonely life, guilty of some unforgivable personal atrocity.

At the funeral, the line of parishioners
snaked outside the gates of the cemetery,
stunned at the event that has left them wondering
does God still hear their prayers or is this the death of divinity?

The crows now roost in what has
once again become the hanging tree,
above the headstones beneath which,
it is said, all God's creatures rest in peace.

While the Inspector Chief and his followers
meet beneath the new moon of a vacant night
to worship the darkness they have brought into their midst,
in exchange for gifts and the promise of eternity.

Salem Liberation

Manuel Pérez-Campos

Eat sourly, my love, enragèd husband
of a dead decade: with this stew kettled
for you in the abyss of my well-kept
hearth be claimed by dawn-picked herbs that will soon
blunt your waking. You are tame now, you are
sub-putrescently rubescent: kindly
allow me with this athame to open
the fountain of your carotid, that I
may drink your failing health in my rosette
cup. I am become a Maenad this new
moon; I am become Pan's vadelect: I
will hang you from a hook in the larder
lean-to; and that I may consolidate
my bond with the things of earth, I will eat
the worms that from your orifices sprout.

Herpetology

F. J. Bergmann

After *The Smoking Room*, oil on panel, Kelli Hoppman, 2017

Call your parasol a nightshade if it offers any
protection from the baleful effects of cosmic
radiation. Those such as yourself are immune
to moonlight even when it dances on water.
Though robed in human raiment, it is quite clear
what you have become. Your companion is now
your lawful prey. Smoke rising from the brazier
in the bottom of the boat won't save him. Stars
like snake's eyes crouch in immobile grass, coil
in branches lacing lakeshore lawns with shadow.
No one watches from the distant, mapled bluffs.
Despite lingering twilight, your appetite is ravenous.
The lap of waves suggests that you wet your lips,
unhinge your jaw, extend your forked tongue.

The Witches' Rite at Beltane

(a poem in quinta rima, an invented form)

Frank Coffman

Through the barren trees
The sun, blood-red, a devil's eye,
With veins of black, stares down on pagan rite
A witches' coven—now a cry
Is born on the cold breeze.

And all the forms of Night
Descend upon the land. The Dark
Is only one; another is the chill;
Another Hell's itself—Hark!
There! In the waning light!

Cresting the nearby hill,
Descending to unholy chants,
A black-horned Demon sweeps on bat-like wings
Into the circle of the witches' dance.
The hags, cavorting still,

Surround the fiend. One clings—
With pale arms flung about its neck—
This chosen one will be the Hell-spawn's bride.
Each year this night, at the coven's beck,
This ceremony brings

Such a union. Each Beltane-tide,
When seeding the year's next crops is done
A demon comes to seed a witch's womb.
She'll walk, ere many seasons run,
Her Hellion by her side.

. . . . .

Full many Evils loom,
Plaguing our way through this Vale of Tears.
This demon-summoning, damned, abysmal rite:
But adds one more to our deepest fears
On the journey toward the tomb.

The Old Ones: A Ghazal

Joshua Gage

The ocean echoes with the spells that impound the Old Ones.
Upon this shore in days long gone, that high priest drowned the Old
    Ones.

Can you feel their fury? Can you see the waves turn red?
Can you smell the sailor corpses that surround the Old Ones?

The pages of the ebon tome rustle in the wind.
The mirror has shattered. The fire burns green. We have found the Old
    Ones.

The moon over Innsmouth town is swallowed by the maw of night.
We read the constellations in the stars that crowned the Old Ones.

In his padded cell, the Pilgrim babbles prophecies.
His sanity has come unwound with nightmares that resound with the
    Old Ones.

A note on the form:
The ghazal is a poetic form with roots in the Arabian Peninsula. It is arguably the oldest poetic form still in use today. Pre-Islamic Arab poets created the form that is now known as the ghazal in the eighth and ninth centuries, codifying the rules of meter and form, and separating it as a distinct poetic form from other similar forms. While there were many translations of classical ghazals in English throughout the twentieth century, it was not understood as a form until Agha Shahid Ali introduced the rules of the ghazal to the English language in the 1980s.

A ghazal is a poem written in couplets with a strict meter. The distinguishing element of the ghazal is the rhyme and refrain combination. The first couplet of the poem establishes a rhyme and refrain combination, as both lines end with this identifying mark. Successive couplets maintain the form with the second line of each couplet maintaining the rhyme and refrain combination. Furthermore, it is imperative that the couplets stand alone as unique entities, different from and unrelated to the other couplets around it. Agha Shahid Ali often compared each couplet to a bead in a necklace—unique and beautiful on its own, but given greater meaning when put together with other beads. The final rule for the ghazal is that the ending couplet must have a signature from the poet in some way, whether this be a pseudonym or a pen name, or even a direct statement of the name.

Last Ascent

Ann K. Schwader

Among the rubble that a jungle makes
of man & his ambitions, tumbled stones
marked out the mercy rendered by a quake
that shattered earth & sky & blood & bone
alike: a pyramid of sacrifice
surrendered to its dark gods in a trice.

Its stairs worn concave by unwilling feet
still bore the chronicles of wizard-kings
long nameless. Tainted. Even in defeat—
writ *death*–such wisdom wrought a reckoning
upon some future generation, paid
by those too ignorant to be afraid.

Their first discoverer knew little more
than grasping after wonders. Scholarship
soon paled to acquisition as the lore
of centuries fell silent in his grip
that stacked & packed, but never even tried
to crack these shadowed glyphs before he died.

Catalogued, forgotten, locked away
from lesser intellectuals who might
aspire to curiosity, they stayed
as safe as terrors may. Yet elder Night
still thirsted after what it once received
upon those sanguine steps when men believed.

In whispers slipped between the ribs of dreams
that starving scholars pray for (unaware
the void may answer), it deployed its scheme
against our world. Ambition's twisted snare
soon settled on an epigraphic dunce
who seized his opportunity at once.

No mortal mind still living held the key
to those inscriptions, until midnight brought
strange inspiration. Though ability
had hobbled him for decades, he forgot
frustration in translating, without flaw,
this fatal fracturing of cosmic law.

Soon words alone did not suffice. To raise
the thing itself became his single goal
& full-time occupation. As each day
disclosed the next, he barely felt his soul's
blood mingling with the mortar to attract
the awful Patron of this artifact.

At last, as final risers clawed against
a sky too small & clean to comprehend
their heresies, he shivered with a sense
of something waiting. *Someone*. To defend
his life seemed less than futile. Stair by stair,
he rose into the ravening dark air.

Morbidezza

Manuel Arenas

Immured within a tourmaline tower, the Vampiress Morbidezza
Vespertilio waits. Weary and wan, she gazes through the silver bars at the
crimson-colored glass of the lone tower window that keeps the
deleterious sunlight at bay. Combing her silken sable tresses, she broods
over her dispossession and personal losses as she tries to recall the aspect
of spilt blood on a moonlit kill. She is allowed one book by her captor; a
Bible, which she largely ignores save for when she uses it as a *sors
sanctorum* to divine auguries of her coveted escape. To while away the
endless hours of her captivity, she plays her spinet and sings a
melancholy monody for her lost love, Körbl Graf von Totenlaut, who
was slain by Adalbert Glöde, a towheaded prosperous blacksmith's son
and self-styled vampire hunter from Leipzig. He staked the venerable
count as he lay, estivate and defenseless in his coffin, then decapitated
him and stuffed his mouth with garlic. However, when it came time to
dispatch his Venetian consort, beauty stayed the slayer's hand.

The inexpert young Adalbert was so taken by her luxuriant black hair,
her exquisite pallor and scarlet mouth, that he could not bring himself to
destroy her. Instead he bound her coffin in silver chains and kept it under
a haystack in his father's smithy until he could build a small tower house
with schorl transported from the Ore Mountain Range in Saxony, which
he furnished with some of her belongings that he seized from the
vampire's schloss. He erected the structure deep in a riparian forest, far
away from prying eyes, and placed its entrance on the banks of the river so
that if the lady found her way out of her confinement, she could not cross
the threshold. The somber tower loomed forbiddingly beneath the crown
canopy of the forest like a benighted beacon. Its piceous walls were barely
capable of retaining the mortiferous miasma that seeped between its
stones through the porous mortar, blighting the adjacent demesne; felling
all the flora save for deadly nightshade, and repelling all the fauna save for

those creatures that emerge after the vesper bells summon the faithful to eventide orisons; most notably a cortège of bats, which swarmed the structure, flying to the aid of their sovereign.

To curry favor with the lady, and at considerable cost to his already depleted purse, he purchased an ornate girandole mirror from her native land, replete with candlesticks to light up her gloomy little chamber. When she espied it across the room, upon awakening from her diurnal repose, the lady overlaid it apace with a cramoisy mantle that suggested to him a cascade of blood. Abashed upon grasping his gaffe, he left for her a turtledove in a gilded cage as a peace offering, only to discover upon the morrow the headless, bloodless body of the little bird sprawled within the mangled cage. Conceding defeat, he swore off procuring anything else for the dark donna that she did not herself request.

Because his Lutheran sensibilities won't allow for the procuration of human blood for her profane sustenance, she has become etiolate, torpid, and, to all appearances, exanimate. Yet underneath that lifeless façade her preternatural anatomy toils constantly to revivify her undead carcass as her demoniac mind cogitates on vendetta. Unsure of how to gauge her condition, Adalbert visits his captive daily in her solitary room and lights a spermaceti candle by her catafalque so that he may pore over her comely countenance, looking for signs of corruption whilst furtively pining for a return of her unnatural vigor.

For hours he gapes at her black velvet voluptuousness and her necrophilic allure: her alabaster bosom, her pallid brow, and her mesmeric red mouth. The gelid touch of her marmoreal flesh causes a thrilling horripilation to surge through his piqued physique. Every day he stays longer and longer, lingering until his eyes start to grow bleary and flutter as the candle flame sputters into oblivion in a puddle of pellucid wax. And all the while Morbidezza's violet spherules, ostensibly insensate, peer surreptitiously through the villous lashes of her creviced eyelids, awaiting the day when her besotted subduer tarries too long in his vigil, providing her an opportunity to exact her revenge under the sanguinary rays of the setting sun as it filters through the crimson panes of the tower window like a cataract of retributive blood.

Life Decayed

Ashley Dioses

The icy hands that steal
The life-force out of you
Have now upheld their deal;
You join the Reaper's queue.

The darkness stole your hope,
And all your dreams were shattered.
Nothing could help you cope;
Your life was then left tattered.

Your silky, softened skin
Had turned so green and sour.
You let the darkness in,
So slowly, hour by hour.

For you, it is too late.
Alone, you have been picked.
It was left up to Fate;
Your clock its last has ticked.

Your time has just run out;
What else is left to do
Than leave without a doubt
That this was right on cue?

At last, the Reaper came
As you lay there afraid.
The ravens sought to claim
Your corpse, a life decayed.

Lord of Pumpkins

Scott J. Couturier

Into the patch I gleefully go,
to fix my roots, to coil & grow.

Lord of Pumpkins, once Man I was:
now the omnipresent insect buzz
o'er luxuriant vines is dearly mine.
Through grass my greening tendrils twine.

Into the patch I gleefully go,
to fix my roots, to coil & grow.

Once Man, now vegetable I am.
But more: a Lord of Fields I am.
Of rot & mold & loamy wind
& the oatmeal-chest o'er-brimmed—
I am husk-rustle of each elfin leaf
as chill wind strikes at bowers brief.

Into the patch I gleefully go,
to fix my roots, to coil & grow.

The Dead all know me by my Name—
they dance 'round me a circle game.
Yet, hollow my flesh & put a candle in
& they flee exalting from my grin!
A hallowed god of olden Ways—

the squeal of sawing fiddle plays
as scythes dissever old Barley John:
the Season's come, & the Season's gone.

Into the patch I gleefully go,
to fix my roots, to coil & grow.

Once Man, my flesh was coarse to me.
A means to shed it sought I endlessly.
Fruitless quest, 'til Pan's luscious lute
summoned me forth to *become* Fruit.
Now splay I gloating in summer's heat
as autumn creeps nigh on stealthy feet:
below, the dead twitch impatient bones.
The skewed bulks of worn gravestones
lie heavy on each unsettled wight
yearning year-round for that Night of nights.

Into the patch I gleefully go,
to fix my roots, to coil & grow.

Lord of Pumpkins, once Man was I:
But no more Man. Pumpkin am I.

(*For K. A. Opperman*)

Nighttime Visitor
Where Cats Prowl

For Brenley

Randall D. Larson

You wake to darkness
Something moving beside you
A menacing growl.

The dim pre-dawn light
Reveals a country landscape
Dim-litten houses.

Fleeing the covers
Your eyes dart around the room
Nothing moves, sounds gone.

Then, stillness shattered . . .
It comes again, softly smooth
A delicate purr . . .

A cat? In this inn?
In your room, here in this place?
Prowling, stalking you?

You recall old tales
Of travelers robbed or slain
By wicked nomads.

Or those who kept cats
Large, wickedly fanged and clawed
To do their killing.

You recall again
The sound that woke you from sleep
Were you, true, alone?

Or did a footstep
Wake you *first*, leaving the room
Your purse in their hand?

Again a growl heard
A shifting of the blankets
Then a shadow leapt.

It, like dark syrup,
Flowed out into the morning
Silently and gone

Glance. Your purse remained
A theft not yet completed.
But what of that cat?

You cross to the hall
Padding feet like clouds on stone
You follow the sound.

Down the hall a door
Hangs open, a salty stench
Warns you of spilt blood.

Fellow traveler
His purse empty, abandoned
His neck severed, cold.

Another one lies
Bloody, beside him; torn, clawed
Dead hands clutch jewels.

Recompense received
The thief never made escape
But what of the cat?

Head shaking, you leave
But a new sight haunts your mind,
Vexing your worries.

A large cat, scruffy,
Licking blood off its grey fur
Its eyes glimmering

As it watches you
Emerge into morning's chill
And tread out of town.

Unease weighs heavy
You pass empty homes barren
But for watchful cats.

Your worry calms and
You feel comfort from those toms
And you understand.

You may return here
For this town harbors shelter
For the wanderer.

Through the gentle sound
A cat's purr, reassuring
They will protect you.

Unnatural Man

Mary Krawczak Wilson

The snow is dotted in ash—so black
Like pepper flakes on an egg—so white.
And when I saw you:
Your eyes were aflame and eerily bright
And pierced me blind in your acidic attack.

The sky is bleeding and hemorrhaging red
Like clots of rose petals now burnt pink.
And when I felt you:
Your hand was as heavy as a metallic link
That twisted around my malformed head.

The ocean is bleached out and blue
Like dungarees once new, now gray.
And when I heard you:
Your voice echoed from Himalayan peaks far away,
Deafening me in its explosive invidious way.

The moon is wafer-thin and brown
Like a stagnant pond, once green.
And when I succumbed to you:
Your teeth were sharp, jagged, and unclean
And cauterized me as I lay, lifeless, on the ground.

One Who Walks Alone

Carl E. Reed

The castle dark loomed tall & stark
upon the stony hill
where nothing green would grow but black
nettles, mold & chill
fungoid forms: mottled stalks
supporting toxic heads
mushroom in shape & oozing vile
ichors o'er undead
ghoulish forms entombed below
that neither laugh nor weep,
but shuffle-moan through crypt & tunnel
dank & fathoms deep.

I started up the flagstone path,
a whisper in the night;
the blood-red gibbous moon above
shone down its fulgent light.
No stranger I to castle dark;
not guest, but rather, host
of many an eldritch ritual there:
Warlock, scholar, ghost.
I wept & walked with straited gait;
I strode that path alone.
Burnt at the stake long ages past,
I reclaimed my ancient home.

When the Nightwind Howls

Leigh Blackmore

(*In Memoriam Michael Fantina*)

He dreamt of realms forsaken
Beneath swart midnight skies;
Of men by dooms o'ertaken,
And lovers' joyful cries.

He glimpsed far Nithon's flowers;
Their blooms so weird he sang in note
As though from distant bowers
Where nightingales give throat.

With velvet gowns and silky
That draped unearthly shapes
Of luscious maidens milky,
Reclining, eating grapes,

His visions filled his pages;
With silver and with gold;
With tales of ancient ages
And heroes swift and bold;

He dreamt of worlds forgotten;
Colossal planets, vast;
And creatures ill-begotten
From aeons, ages past;

And when we hear the nightwind
A-howling in the eaves,
And when dusky noon turns light-dimmed,
His muse will make blood freeze.

He sang far lands and starlight;
He sang weird loves obsessed;
And when we sense a far light
We think long on his quest

To bring the realms of fancy
Within each reader's grasp—
To limn the realms of shadows
In lines that make us gasp.

His wizardry is ended—
His magic yet lives on.
His course, though now it's wended,
Will never be quite gone.

Going Forth by Night

Margi Curtis

There is a place Between where shadows fall,
Between the sun and moon, between light rays,
Where I can just discern a distant call
That stirs my heart to shed familiar ways
And, risking all, let star-dark presence draw
Forth holy dread, now knocking at my door.

And if I open to that nameless one
Whose breath reminds me of a rhyme scarce heard,
And if I glimpse her fingers pale as bone
Or smell the scorch of purgatory herb,
Might I not fall, surrender to her charm,
Convincing me that Change can do no harm?

I cannot see it clear, that place Between
From where no one I know has yet returned
Unscarred, unheard, unmade or yet unseen,
Unrecognisable, for they have learned
The truth about that presence, about pain,
And what it means to die and live again.

Withal, I sit here, spellbound by this sound
And gaze into the shadows, breathless, still.
I listen for the song of sky and ground,
Of frogs, of owls and bats both soft and shrill.
I take up my guitar and pluck a string—
And far off now I hear the witches sing.

After the Cryptozoic

Kendall Evans

After the Cryptozoic Era
the platypus stopped dancing with the monkey-squirrel
no more tango for two or roundelu
no more pteranodons flew with the gulls

meanwhile volcanoes belched and roared their gall
the earth quaked, and the ground shook resoundingly—

and we two, you and I, in our simian guises/disguises
tap-danced our way around our planet's circumference
treading carefully

The Assignment

Liam Garriock

(*Inspired by the films of Jan Svankmajer, the surrealist of Prague*)

Instructed by higher forces to assassinate a man who had caused great disruption to our country, I made my way into the very heart of the bleak and lonely countryside, at the very edge of our poor and repressed nation. This man, who shall remain nameless like the forces that authorized his termination, had, as I have said, infuriated our nation, for he utilised the marvellous powers of the uncanny to breathe life into things that should not live or no longer live. Like a skilled thaumaturge, he animated things as diverse as blankets, toys, fruit, meat, moth-eaten clothes, primordial stones, false teeth, ravenous skulls, stuffed animals, plaintive statues, dolls, paintings, and, worst of all, corpses. There was not a thing in the country that did not jitter or quiver or stir into an ephemeral life at this enigmatic magician's touch. This activity, this deeply unforgivable activity in the eyes of many, had affronted the government of our deeply conservative nation.

"Annihilate the alchemist! Destroy the demiurge! Murder the magician!" my people shouted, terrified of whatever commonplace household apparatus might suddenly begin to move on its own accord and dance across the dusty wooden tables.

I was tasked with finding the magician and destroying him, for I was trained in the art of eliminating the undesirables of our society; many an artist and a penniless poet had met his end at my pistol, and, like men walking to the gallows, they never protested. Now that our country was on the verge of descending into hallucinatory chaos, it was up to me to keep our staid values and hoary traditions alive. We manage to trace him to a lonely house in a desolate expanse of countryside where the trains never passed and the rivers ran black with filth. I made my way through that grey and sombre landscape, with its foggy, reed-choked swamps and marshes, its barren fields, its dead trees, until I found myself at the decayed and looming edifice of the metaphysician. Entering, I found that all the rooms were empty, but in one room upstairs, peering by the open door, I found my target. I espied the sequestered magician work his magic. Tarot cards slid across the table on their own, crumpled scraps of paper arranged and rearranged themselves into numerous shapes like protean lifeforms, dusty china dolls with frozen expressions performed strange dramas, homunculi grew from Lilliputian skeletons to fully formed infants and adults, and an apple jumped and rolled around in agony as maggots ate away at its core. All these and more were the enemies of our nation, and it was my duty to extinguish them forever.

Yet, as I raised my silenced pistol to the aged magician's head, who certainly saw me yet made no effort to escape or beg for his life, I saw him begin to animate a group of toy children the size of a man's head; they were playing a miniature game of football with a glass eye on the gnarled table of wood, bickering, tripping over one another, embracing each other like friends. For a moment I forgot my duty and who sent me, but, as I stood enraptured, the children felt to the floor, inert, swept away by an invisible force to make way for the next spectacle. This time it was two human skulls, gazing at each other, circling suspiciously, fraught with uncertainty; after a moment, they seemed to be kissing each other, their bleached teeth touching; then they opened their mouths, allowing a worm that acted as a living tongue to snake out and wrap around each other. This macabre love story then made way for the next show: in the corner, a life-sized skeleton stood as though awaiting something, then clay appeared to dress it, to give it muscle and sinew and tissue, before the flesh of clay wriggled off it to leave it a bare skeleton once again.

During these miniature wonders, I was a child once again. But the harsh voices of stern authority barked into my head and ordered me to kill the man responsible for these "obscenities." Without hesitating, I fired my pistol straight at the magician's head. A bloody, bleeding hole appeared in his forehead, like a crimson portal into the mind that spawned these strange and uncanny marvels, before he fell onto his table, dead. All the objects in this room ceased to function along with their master: the toy children never kicked the eyeball again, the death-head lovers never displayed any affection towards each other again, the skeleton in the corner quickly gave up any hope of ever gaining skin again. The house was dead this time, utterly dead.

Having done my duty, I left the empty, gloomy house and made my way through the haunted, gloomy country, to the city of crushed dreams where my superiors coldly congratulated me, in a land of false promises and stillborn hopes.

A Ride in Hilo

Chad Hensley

On the airliner, there was a very small boy
With six fingers on each hand and six toes on each foot.
He moved up and down the aisle with an uncanny ease,
Swinging up into his parents' arms,
His tiny face engulfed with a soft, unbridled fury
And enormous smile.

In the seat across the aisle from mine
Sat his father—short blond hair and stocky frame
With terrible neck tattoos and oversized baseball cap.
His mother was a petite Pacific Islander
With long raven hair and piercing brown eyes,
Forced to sit four seats up due to an error.

One thing Dad liked to do was drink.
He was nice enough already, chatting it up
As the child ran up and down the aisle during the flight,
Back and forth between mother and father,
Leaping and landing perfectly each time
As if he'd done it a thousand times before.

When I bought a round with my frequent flyer coupons,
Dad said he was going to meet his wife's side of the family for the first time.
When his speech wandered to "fishing, fighting, and fucking"—
'His three favorite things'—and that he was getting ready to do a lot of those
It didn't really faze me; I liked to drink as well

And I had come to respect his blunt construction worker worldview
Peppered with just enough bits of California punk
That his conversation was worth encouraging just a few times.

But what bothered me the most
Was the sound of his voice
When he spoke about the family members he hadn't met before.

When we landed on the island, I said a cordial
"Nice to meet you, goodbye" to the mom and dad,
Smiled at the kid and got off the plane.

After fetching my luggage and a short bus ride
To get the rent-a-car (a 4x4 Jeep, btw)
I drove for two hours through lava fields
That looked like endless miles of cratered moon,
A black and glistening sheen here and there, now and then,
Great expanses of wild grasses fighting with the rock for hold upon the earth.

I could not see the sky as a steady rainfall began
Thick gray clouds engulfing the road in all directions.
Sometimes, patches of dense jungle came into view
Filled with verdant plants and palms I'd never seen before.

I reached the dock
Just as an enormous red sun was starting to set over the ocean waters.

The first crew member I saw
Was a middle-aged, short, bald and obese Hawaiian.
He was barefoot, and his very large toe nails
(enormously overgrown, curved, sharpened, and dirty yellow)
Looked like medieval weapons.
His cylinder-like legs were fat, muscular cankles covered with furry green patches
Of what looked like barnacles, or maybe lichens
That I've seen growing on century-old Magnolias in deep south bayous.

His belly, shoulders, and back where covered with thick, black lines
With what I thought at first were intricately detailed tribal tattoos
Until I realized it was all a vast ocean
With dozens of giant octopus tentacles undulating in the splashing waves.
Like a star burning in outer space, a gargantuan starfish with a single glowing eye
And impossibly long spiny arms was submerged,
Tiny humanoids swimming around it.
On a craggy beach above, the tops of giant wooden pillars driven into the rock
Had been carved into gilled human-like heads,
White caps pounding the shoreline.

As the man hobbled around the dock,

He easily unwound thick corded rope
From chiseled cleats driven into concrete with massive iron nails.
I was pleased to see the other crew members looked (almost) normal, one
    of the deck hands was even from Pensacola, Florida, and I'd been
    there many times.

I took a seat on the right-hand side in an empty row near the back
That gave me a great view of the ocean,
Though there were several other passengers onboard.

It was an hour of rough seas (and a few tourists vomited)
Before we came upon the spot
Where the lava poured into the dark, churning waters—
Fiery black rock flowed like giant play-dough snakes,
Glowing bright hues of reds and oranges,
Sputtering and spurting great amounts of steam and hot debris
As the burning coils slithered into the sea.

In the distance (if you looked hard), you could see the coning tip
Of what the locals were calling Fissure 8—
A wide crack in the earth that spewed a molten river
Downhill and into the ocean.

Amidst the clicking of cameras and cell phones,
Along with a few 'Oohs' and 'Ahs' from the passengers,
There was another sound—almost like a heartbeat.

Suddenly a great mewing arose,
And out of the corner of my eye
I saw a massive undulating shadow
And then the fat and tattooed crew member
Dove head first into the churning, steaming waters
From the back of the boat.

No one else seemed to see any of this.
The other crew members frowned at me
As the boat headed back to the dock.

But there was a point just as we were leaving the spot
When I looked back.
On a far shore of jagged, black rocks
Dozens of shapes danced
In the mist of crashing waves just across from the thick walls of rising
    smoke.
I know I saw an oversized ball cap on backwards
On the head of one of the revelers,
Though many of them looked like they were not wearing clothes.

But what was far more disturbing
Was what appeared to be a naked, bald fat man
Riding upon a cuttlefish the size of a horse
As the creature jumped out of the dark waters,
Larger shadows moving beneath.

Supernumerary

Mike Allen and S. Brackett Robertson

You're forty when your new teeth grow in.
They halt your speech,
English and Spanish both turn strange on your tongue,
tripping against the new walls.

But now, it seems, you can hear the stars.

You try to tune them out sometimes,
when sounds spin asymmetrical,
rattle discordant in your throat.

And yet you have the urge to join their song,
croon with the sky, attempt mimicry,
though your vocal cords and tongue
can't quite accommodate
the requisite multi-track glossolalia.

These new teeth are at least attuned
if not in tune, needles pressing on
metaphysical vinyl the way fangs scrape bone,
the vocabulary dictated by the dim blackboards
of your palm-tree, spider-web childhood
scraped and scrambled on the turntable.

(You've mostly forgotten the other children's voices,
raised in mocking cacophony.

You had no extra teeth then,
and still they thought you strange.)

The mirror shows you blunted incisors
and molars in a single simple row, but your finger
traces more, three rows, four, a spiral draining
toward your throat. You must conclude
they grew from somewhere beyond
space and time and your X-ray defined jaw.

Soon you find the teeth elsewhere,
outside your body altogether, yet a part,
growing at the bottom of your coffee mug,
nestled among the roots of your begonias.

You'd think they bespeak a hunger
that extends to your environment, and for sure
there's a lot of chewing going on
behind your back, given the discarded shells
and skins of untraceable origin you find
lying about your house, the bite marks fresh.

Pieces perhaps picked from the pockets
of other universes, maybe a world
you really come from, where you're not a monster.

Bathysphere

Oliver Smith

Five miles down on the descent: beyond
ruined reefs and melt-drowned peaks;
at three tons per square inch
the red glow of burning seamounts,
smoked black the boiling water.
In darker fissures below soot filled seas
eels paled at a glimpse of yellow light;

on a thread the crane unspooled:
pitched and yawed on the pendulum steel
and plumbed the waves with a shell
whose rivet and weld refused to weep
for tender flesh inside. The crewman
had an incompressible urge for the deep
as he unwound the steady winch—

fishy dragons blinked with swollen eyes
that chased down the falling capsule;
their silver flesh surrounded
by bluely luminous satellites.
Deeper still on the abyssal brink
life burned twice as bright where
translucent stars made galaxies

in the artificial twilight.
Insatiable hunger all head and belly
blazed in monstrous passions;
signals flashed coded from Leviathan's
jewelled flesh; older than stardust
dreaming in the inky darkness;
blinking slow in space-deep sleep.

Illuminated in the cabin's electric glow
the faces of curious mariners swam
sedately past or waved and called;
knocked on the steel walls and mouthed
questions about their abandoned families,
and invited him for a rum and shanty
beyond the porthole of foot thick glass.

The Forsaken Idol

David Barker

Kaleb found the discarded icon in a pile of rubble on the margin of an empty field behind the ruins of an ancient church. Made of stone and as tall as the length of his forearm and hand together, it was noticeably heavy but not so much so that he couldn't carry it. Wrapping the odd figurine in his coat so that none would see him removing a precious relic from a sacred site, Kaleb carried the small statue to his hut and set it upright on the table that served as an altar where he performed his daily meditations. The icon fit in well with the other religious objects that he had assembled over the years, and Kaleb had the impression that it was comfortable in this setting and felt at home there. To keep the icon a secret from the prying eyes of visitors, Kaleb erected a screen around the altar, converting it into a private space that only he would see. Thus did Kaleb begin his tradition of saying prayers to the icon every morning when the first rays of the sun broke above the crest of the jagged volcanic mountains that circled his village and again each night when the lustrous silver beams of moonlight washed over the dense woods and flowered meadows of the slumbering valley. The prayers he uttered in an elder, almost forgotten tongue gave Kaleb an overpowering sense of peace and wholeness, as if he were a part of something much larger than himself— the constellated consciousness of all those who spoke such prayers, laid offerings, and made sacrifices to the eternal god force embodied in the primordial stone idol. But that sense of peace and wholeness was shattered one evening when Kaleb knelt down before the icon and was about to begin his incantation of obedience and praise. For in the shadows of the small, screened-in altar place known only to Kaleb, he was startled to see the icon's two eyes suddenly glowing a fierce red—the ruby radiance of molten lava. Before he could comprehend what was happening, the screen around the private altar was engulfed in flame, and just as instantly the entire hut was burning. Kaleb had no time to gather his humble possessions, not even the most precious items among the few things he could call his own. In moments his dwelling collapsed into burning timbers and straw, and within an hour nothing remained but glowing embers and gray ash. There, under the wreckage of all that he had owned in this world, Kaleb left the scorched stone idol, once again forsaken, where it still awaits the next hopeful man who will find it and believe that he has been blessed.

In the Garden of Thasaidon

Jeff Hall

Gently whispering the five names
Of the demon lord Thasaidon
I step into his own garden
After long days on troubled roads.

Pendulous blood-red fruits abound,
Bursting wantonly with fiery juice
From which to distill a liquor
Potent, burning, diabolic.

Others seek wines from distant lands,
But only a sacred spirit
Can sate my thirst for corruption
And what else lies beyond that cup.

(for Clark Ashton Smith)

The Dark King

Allan Rozinski

Deep in the forest's hidden spaces
where nature's ebb and flow is found,
and decay ferments underground,
here, the pagan rites take place.

The ceremonies held secret as required,
the sacrifices offered—a jealous god's spoils,
blood spills across the altar, then down to the soil,
where life and death merge and conspire.

Each disciple wearing robe and hood
gathers round countless bodies grown cold,
bled dry to summon The Dark King of old
that now menaces from the nearby wood.

Its head crowned with a bed of writhing vines,
gnarled branches for limbs, a trunk-body massive in size;
the ground rumbles and quakes with each step it takes, its eyes
reflecting apocalyptic warning signs.

The ritual resumes at their strange messiah's command
to poison the fount of hope and thwart the unseeing drive
toward the futile future to which the wretches still strive
—this has always been The Dark King's plan.

The Offspring

Barbara Barrett

My mother was a werewolf,
My father an old vampire.
Except for sharply pointed teeth
There wasn't a better sire.

An accident—it's what I am—
Between two bestial beasts
Who took a little R & R
From hunting human feasts.

'Twas the union of all unions.
The trees will never grow back;
Eerie spirits still dance around,
And the ground will ever be black.

Wolf howls filled our dusty halls.
The bats all flew with Dad.
I slept all day and played each night.
Such happy times we had!

Our favorite game was hide and seek,
And they searched high and low
While I hid in the greenhouse shed
Beneath the sunlamp's glow.

Then silver bullets hit their mark.
And I miss my family.
Still, those slayers were awf'ly good.
Delicious and savory.

The Mirror of Arkham Woe

or, Marginalia in the Book of Revelation from Nahum Gardner's Bible

Manuel Pérez-Campos

The alkahest of the well-scorching colour
has tainted it too so that its plain oval
frame returns to her a rutilant face
half-eaten by arabesques of worms, those
usherers of our sons' futurity.
Lock'd in the attic, all she does is mourn,
in the dull regalia of her bridal
noon, our farmstead in it shorn of lustre
like a black emerald—& worse: inflam'd
by nightside reason to eldritch agony.
I have glimps'd her thro' the door's peephole,
transfix'd by the madden'd rush of centuries
beaming out of it with the velocity
of dream; & trembled when she was condemn'd
to screech & float, bereft of will to spurn
the silvery tentacles of its embrace.

A reader's interpolated extension to
H. P. Lovecraft's "The Colour out of Space."

The Driver of the Dragon's Coach

Wade German

He comes at evening or when twilight falls,
His horses silent, gliding on the night.
And all who witness cross themselves on sight,
Knowing he hastens to his master's call
As if a demon, summoned by black mass.
They say his face forever is the same,
That none have ever learned his Christian name—
Thus call him Charon of the Borgo Pass:

For souls his coach collects do not return,
But travel roads where weird blue witch-lights burn
As *he* communicates with wolf and ghost
That guard the ebon gate to Dracul's keep—
Where passengers become unholy host
At feasts for dragons, wakened from their sleep.

Mad Jack-a-Lee

Adam Bolivar

Mad Jack-a-Lee to Hexham came
    With blood upon his boots;
The laws of men could never tame
    The wildness in his roots.

At crossing roads he found an inn,
    And thought to take a drink;
From travelling he was bone-thin—
    A skeleton you'd think.

Inside the inn was thick with smoke,
    A noxious swirling haze;
Jack strode across the creaking oak
    And caught the barman's gaze.

"A pint of ale or maybe two,"
    He said as cold as ice.
"My name is Jack, I say to you;
    Don't make me say it twice."

A balladress upon the stage
    Strummed on a black guitar,
Emballading Jack's scarlet rage,
    As she watched from afar.

"And for this ale how will you pay?"
    The barman asked of Jack,
And no more words would e'er he say,
    For came a pistol's crack.

The barman's blood ran dark and red,
    Like wine that had been spilled,
And now he lay, his spirit fled,
    The latest Jack had killed.

Jack lay his gun upon the bar,
    And helped himself to rye;
He thought of those he'd killed in war,
    The men he'd left to die.

The balladress was hot as flame,
    And burned for love of Jack,
Though never would he feel the same—
    His heart was cold and black.

A devil came to steal Jack's soul,
    A woman crimson dressed;
Her eyes were cruel and black as coal,
    And lily was her breast.

Jack stopped and turned a merry dance—
    You should have heard them moan;
It made the singer turn askance,
    And feel then all alone.

And when this wicked deed was done,
    No silver coin was paid;
Jack took in hand his iron gun
    And shot the crimson maid.

The balladress resumed her tune,
    And caught Jack by the eye;
He left her there beneath the moon,
    The one who didn't die.

The Dutchman

Frank Coffman

"I believe I only live to speak this tale—
'Tis sure there's no one else alive to tell
About that voyage to the Gates of Hell.
I've seen her! Saw her hoving in full sail
Straight down upon us, suddenly appearing!
And on her decks—Oh! what a ghastly view!
All skeletons made up that hideous crew!
Grim, at her wheel, that cursèd captain steering:
'May I be damned if we'll head into anchor!
We'll round the Cape, or may we never land
Until the Day of Judgment is at hand!'
So cried out Van der Decken in his rancor.
    That Ghost Ship sailed right through us abroadside
    And then moved on across the black waves wide.

We all stood watching her, agape, aghast—
Grey, yet transparent as she faded quite
Into the darkness of that moonless night—
And tossed about by the moaning wild wind's blast
Her tattered sails and broken mizzen mast
Gave further proof to us of the omen dire:
That those who see her will—quite soon—expire.
And, suddenly, with only moments passed,

I stood in horror: my shipmates one by one
Dropped to the deck down dead— Yes! Everyone!
All, all but me. I am the very last.
    I swear The Dutchman's real—you must believe!"
    Then he died, wild-eyed, with only me to grieve.

The Light at the End of the Tunnel

Christina Sng

We take turns to hold Papa
As we make our way
Through the dark tunnel

In search of the other side,
A promise of new life, far from
The broken world we left behind.

The long night is almost over.
We see a shimmer of light
At the end of the tunnel.

Is it real or just a mirage, Papa asks.
We have been mistaken
Many times already.

Once it was fireflies, trapped
In the tunnel along with us.
Another time, a discarded torch

And its owner, shrunken
And broken beside it, its hand
Holding a photograph

Of a smiling happy family,
A thing of the past, since
The world fractured in two.

We press on, staying close
Together, dragging our dying
Water stores and dried food

To what may be our only hope,
The sanctuary at the end.
But now we sleep again,

Huddling together as we did,
In another age,
When Papa helped me hold Jack

While I cared for Eva,
In Grandma's tiny cabin
By the edge of the woods,

The only place safe from
The monsters that invaded
Our world and slaughtered

The rest of our family.
Now it is Jack who holds Papa
And Eva who holds me,

As the light ahead brightens
And we awake with hope
For the first time in years.

I see the glisten in Papa's eyes,
The hope that he will see Mama again
After all this time

When we took separate routes
To escape the attack on our cabin
One unexpected night.

He hastens our pace,
Discards the walking stick
We made him.

Jack can barely hang on to him.
I grasp his other arm while
Eva drags our supplies.

Lights seeps into every corner,
Every pore of our beings.
It is blinding.

And there lies hope,
In the thick wood and fruit trees,
The throng of people waiting

To see if their loved ones
Have made it through the tunnel.
And there,

An old woman holding
Two small children with my face
Beams like sunshine

As they race to us,
Clasping us tight.
We are finally home.

Gargoyle

Manuel Arenas

How many years have I crouched upon my haunches on this corbel, overlooking the roofs of this tiny village? Who knows; who tracks time but mortals? I have borne the wind's great gusts, with its once refreshing, but now fetid breath; as well as the torrential rainstorms that have lashed about my face, mocking my immobility. But I have endured it all with indifference, for I am imperturbable.

I am a sentinel placed here centuries ago, by men long gone, for a purpose long forgotten by their scions. Forsaken but undaunted, I continue in my service: the duty of guarding these creatures from the ever-present cloud of darkness that hovers over their fragile little heads. Waiting for a chance to slip into this plane from its netherworld of chaos to wreak havoc and obfuscate the eyes of the masses with its visions of wickedness and self-importance.

Preying first on the weaker minds, whose already opaque eyes will be the first to be blinded by its lies. Those who are strong-willed, and resist, will be struck down like bothersome pests, not to be tolerated, much the lass feared.

Thus I await the day with much anticipation when my companions and I shall answer to the call to battle the legions of the dark. Only then shall we have fulfilled our promise to the long-forgotten masons of our visage.

To a Black Hole

Charles Lovecraft

Thou greedy black hole—to drink all the light!
Neutrinos travel, still are snaveled up;
Red dwarves are to you just a little bite;
Drain magellanics in your noxious cup.
I feel the tug of your great terror come
Upon me like soft lowering ropes of night,
And find you are that night of dreams the sum
Which drained away and never had our sight.

Remote your flowing eyes of horror fill,
With motes of streaming constellations, full
Of stars, that sift down steadily, until
You've gorged them all and to the farthest lull,
And I turn speck of dust and fry, a sty—
A nothing scratching your black monster's eye.

All Will Taste Death

Ross Balcom

all will taste death,
all will taste it

ghastly skeletons
collapse in a heap

a still-life
orgy of bone

crawling among them
come the perverts

licking dem bones
licking dem bones

I among them
poet and fiend

wide-eyed
drooling and mad

licking dem bones
spouting dem poems

all will taste death,
but to me

it tastes best

The Birth of Brahma

Rich Catalano

While still the earth was but a half-formed thought,
 And the countless suns in ancient darkness slept;
When godlike Silence reigned and Time was naught,
 I yet was young and in my bosom kept

The eons. In boundless solitude I dwelt,
 Alone with wide-winged Rapture sweet and vast;
Till by My throne a million Powers knelt,
 Each one Myself in Yearning's likeness cast.

And thus took form the wonder-dream of Life,
 Its passion and its loss My secret gain;
For I am the hidden harmony of Strife
 Death but My blissful smile masked as pain.

In man I veil Myself one day to see
The mortal wed to immortality.

The Frightful Ballad of the Third Lord Boyce

Thomas Tyrrell

October winds, October seas,
Around the ship they seethe and roar.
John Graham, the third Lord of Boyce
Hears a knock on his cabin door.

"With compliments of Captain Spence,
You're wanted on the deck,
To see a sight was never seen
From Cape Town to Quebec.

"Your father's ship has come alongside,
And John Graham, the second Lord
Of Boyce, cries out in a fearful voice
For you to come aboard."

The blood fell from Young Boyce's cheek,
His heart was sore afraid.
"My compliments to Captain Spence,
Sure some mistake is made?

"My father's dead ten years this night,
My father died at sea.
All souls aboard his ship were drowned
In the storms of 'ninety-three."

"And was that ship the Son of Eve
Out of the Port o' Spain?
And did it have a figurehead
Bearing the mark of Cain?

"And is your father a red-haired man
Who stands full six-foot high,
With a blazing cheek and a broken nose
And a hellfire gleam in his eye?"

And then Young Boyce went up on deck
To a crew half-mad with terror,
And looking on his father's face
He knew there was no error.

Old Boyce bestrode the quarterdeck;
His cannons were shotted and rammed.
"I'll have Young Boyce to join my crew!
Though we be cursed and damned,

"A man's own son, when all's said and done,
Should stand beside his sire.
So have Young Boyce conveyed aboard,
Or else I'll open fire,

"And the salt sea-waves will be your graves
And your daughters and widows will grieve."
With a single leap, Young Boyce spanned the deep
And stood on the Son of Eve.

Young Boyce went to his father's side
And clasped his outstretched hand,
As fiery red and burning hot
As any cattle brand.

He made his quivering knees be still
He made his heart beat slow
And in a steady, offhand voice,
He asked to go below.

"Oh, my young Boyce, you'll have the choice
Of cabin, as you ought.
A long, long trip you'll spend on ship
Ere we come to any port.

"This night we sail the seas of earth
And feel the fresh west wind.
The Other Place has oceans too,
Though of a different kind,

"With a hot and sulphur-stinking breeze
And a bitter, burning spray,
Where I and you and all our crew
Will sail till Judgment Day."

And then Old Boyce took up his lamp
And led his son below,
Where the lantern's gleams showed only scenes
Of horror, shame, and woe.

But his cabin was filled with gold and jewels,
The spoils of piracy,
With a narrow bunk and a cannon-port
That looked upon the sea.

Here Old Boyce left him to his rest
With the ghastliest of grins,
And Young Boyce, sinking on his bunk,
Bethought him of his sins.

"In Paris and in London I
Have lived a life of pleasure,
Not thinking how my carefree wealth
Was blood-soaked pirate treasure.

"For these bright stones how many bones
Lie bleached and bare and dry?
For wealth untold of Spanish gold
How many men must die?
What comfort can these trinkets give
If I lose my soul thereby?

"Must I share the fate and bear the curse
Of my father and his men?
Oh, I'd rather brave the salt sea-wave,
If my strength should fail—what then?

"Better lose my breath to a sailor's death,
With Davy Jones to dwell,
Than forever ride by my father's side
On the fiery seas of Hell."

And men still speak of the thin white smile
Of his corpse as it lay on the shore,
Like one who's braved Hell's worst and saved
His soul forevermore.

Maculation

F. J. Bergmann

What I missed most were splotches
of color and shade: irregular clouds
above and around me, variegations,
markings, spots, patterns on animals
and plants, even those pale patches
indicating disease. Not a single soul
aboard this ship had even a freckle.

The smooth surfaces, always curved,
swathes of gleaming metal and cool
plastic, were soothing at first, but I
rapidly wearied of glassy expanses
blank as new documents. It had been
decided that viewports might disturb
our focus on expediting the mission,

not to mention fears of what could
inhabit the black void, out in space.
Imaginative activities were strongly
discouraged—and no one wanted to
incur motive enhancement. Fiction
was entirely contraband, but formed
the main currency among our crew.

Then some of us began reporting
visual defects: strange darknesses

that swam before our eyes, stains
spreading over bulkheads, doors,
control panels. Sickbay filled until
we were forbidden from using any
illness to evade our assigned duties.

I and others began guessing as to
how best to adjust those controls
that we could not reliably perceive
any longer—that is, all of them;
we were so accustomed to visuals
that we had neglected touch-marks.
Then tactile input began to deform.

Monsters moved in slowly swirling
blurs, concealing all that lay behind.
We felt their hideous pelts and scales
brush against our skins; we quarreled
endlessly as to whether their textures
were rugose, slimy, or simultaneously
both. We put on blindfolds, gloves . . .

and yet the onslaught did not cease.
We became convinced that beings
had clustered about our ship; that
our only salvation lay in turning

our own weaponry against its hull.
We all volunteered to go outside,
to make the required adjustments.

We put on our spacesuits hastily;
we tore out walls, drilled a passage
when the airlock malfunctioned,
with no thought for atmosphere
or hydroponic gardens. Our terror
was all that mattered. And then
we saw what blotted out the stars.

Bone Riders

Kurt Newton

We cling wetly to
this multi-jointed frame,
riding all day long
through howling wind
and pelting rain,
through sun-filled warmth
beneath clear blue skies,
we ride,
until the damp earth burns
to desert sand,
and daylight turns
to eternal night,
and we leave at last
these bones behind
for a different kind
of journey.

From Spectral Realms

Leigh Blackmore

From spectral realms approach the fearful things
Shapen of mystery, forms of cobweb-grey;
I hear the sounds of vast and beating wings.
From out the storm-tossed sky that blots out day.
Long prisoned in declining earthly flesh,
I onward grope through life with feverish eyes
In search of dreamings that may bring some fresh
Insight—or surcease—careless of its guise.

Cessation of existence, special joy—
Devoutly to be wished, as one might say—
And now these *things* grow near; I am their toy.
Their talons grasp me; I have found the way!
These voiceless, faceless, creatures of the grave
Will bring me the cessation that I crave!

(*For Donald Wandrei*)

Inescapable Horror

Liam Garriock

(A *curious fragment found in an empty flat.*)

I am a tortured soul. When I was a boy, young and naïve, I moved through a verdant grove of wild flowers and creaking alders, and played fanciful games in a rolling meadow. Robins and starlings sang, larks and blackbirds twittered, buzzards and ospreys soared through the deep blue skies, eclipsing the blinding, burning, blazing sun. I rolled down the green and grassy knolls and hillocks, bathing in the sun, breathing in the rich perfumes of the summer flowers, feeling the scintillating splendour of eternity and freedom upon me. But these times I enjoyed alone, for I was a solitary soul, and the company that surrounded me, children my age, I loathed intensely. The more I grew up, the more distant the Arcadian lands became, and the harsher the persecution developed. I was an outcast, a pariah, a scapegoat, and had the eternal mark of Solitude branded on my flesh. Those splendid meadows and fields that I had once loved became grey and ashen and desolate, the flowers dead and withered; the sun which had once shone so strongly became an all-devouring black sun, hanging in a dark and louring sky the colour of livid flesh; the streets where I grew up became deserted and battered by howling winds and smothered in mist.

It was when I was in secondary school that I realised that Paradise, my private, fabled Paradise, never existed. I was surrounded by ugly, monstrous youths and apathetic, glaring adults who cared nothing for our futures. I left school, grew up, and settled in a crushing job in a bleak city that had lost its soul long ago. Those golden days when the sun always shone over eternal Edenic lands seemed long gone and never to return, dead as the empires whose crumbling temples and relics stand like august gravestones amidst impassive people. I was a grievous disappointment of a human being, and my family, who secretly ostracised me, made this very clear. It was not possible to create Paradise, but it was possible to create hell. And that is what we all did: we created hell in our own image, carried it in our hearts everywhere we went, contaminating everything with its demonic ubiquity. I struggled to recreate the Paradise I remembered dimly, but for every flower and every tree, every bird and every bee, darkness ultimately overtook and corrupted. We live in a mass graveyard of slaughtered animals. Our awaiting devil is a chimera whose claws and teeth are crimson with the blood of man and animal alike.

One night, I entered a pub to drown my perennial sorrows, for it was a normal thing to do. I met a comely young woman, spoke to her flatteringly, and took her back to my dishevelled abode. Slightly intoxicated by the liquor, we kissed and undressed and lay on the bed; and, as her naked frame straddled me, I saw, in the moonlit dark of my room, gazing like spectral voyeurs, the charnel wraiths of alchemists, Gnostic visionaries, and seers. They stood motionless like ghoulish statues, watching me with cold and baleful expressions on their mouldering, desiccated faces, judging me, condemning me; and, as I looked up at the young woman, gasping in the throes of ecstasy, I saw that her nubile young body transformed into that of a rotted corpse, her exposed ribcage riddled with maggots and worms that writhed sensually, sharing her hideous orgasm. When I screamed and threw her down to the floor, she cursed indignantly, switched the light on, dressed hastily, and vacated the empty room. I lay on the bed all night, shivering, fearing for my sanity.

After that episode, I lived as a recluse, shunning company, losing my job, dreading that my sanity was going to be ripped away. But, as I grew older, I became acquainted with, and subsequently deeply immersed in, the study of recondite things. Through these studies, I realised that I was not insane, not an aberration in the human race. I lived in an uncanny world that, I understood, had been created with the intention of amassing madness and suffering and cruelty. The deranged and sadistic creator of this carnival of horror, a nameless Demogorgon as elusive as the wind, lay somewhere beyond the diseased universe, beyond time and space. Occasionally its fiendish servants could be glimpsed stalking remote and deserted places, or watching some haunted soul in a public place. I know this because I myself have become a target of these metaphysical ghouls. At first I thought it was my delving into the Delphic secrets of existence that drew their attention to me, but then I realised that they had always been watching me, ever since I was a young boy, playing in those dreamy lands that remain as dead and distant as the fanes and streets of Babylon, and no amount of useless knowledge from rare and forbidden books, no fraudulent mystics, could save me now. My keen sense of injustice was my undoing. I tried to find their point of entry into our world; I travelled to every haunted and lonely region on the maps, but could find only eternal desolation.

It is only a matter of time, now, before they come to collect me. I can sense their shadows falling upon me; I can hear them breathe even though they have no lungs. I know that they are out there, close by, making their move. I could end it now and terminate myself, but I know that they will simply be waiting for me beyond the void. Then again, perhaps there is no powerful Demogorgon. Horrors and abominations exist, but there is no demiurge that controls them. Perhaps CHAOS is the ultimate, immutable EVERYTHING. I shall find out, when they come to claim me, their cold and slimy hands upon me.

Forbidden Fruit

Scott J. Couturier

Forbidden fruit distending from lustrous vine—
about my feet the restless creepers twine.
Upwards peering, gape-mouthed & eyed,
all semblance of self-preservation belied
by the transfixing meat, the sumptuous rind,
of that fruit with which each vine is lined.

Faceted like gems plundered from nobleman's tomb,
each fruit bulges from a hypnotically wavering bloom;
the flowers emit a lulling, insouciant attar
that shears the mind from its crude husk of matter.
Thus transported, the flesh stands in helpless rapport
whilst the hungry tendrils apply their digestive spore.

In this shade-bower, riddled with bones,
I release an ecstatic succession of moans
as the beauteous fruit falls into my hand:
I take a bite in surrender to supernal command.
The taste is sweet, unbearable, divine,
the ardor of infernal suns refined on the vine.

I shiver as my skin dissolves into green-yellow foam,
nostrils choked with the scent of sentient loam.
The fruit-borne bliss sours, a malignant daydream
as I part half-liquid lips to gurgle a scream.
But too late: I am seized in the vines' verdurous hold
& must soon join my kin in the omnipotent mould.

Factotum of the Underworld

David Barker

No master, I,
but rather, slave
to demon lords
who rule the grave.

To hidden crypts
with charms I lure
unwary souls—
the chaste, the pure,

Who will feel a
final shiver
when to foul hands
I deliver.

Forever lost,
these souls naïve
have left behind
loved ones to grieve.

In deepest tombs
vile ghouls debauch,
ravish them as
harpies watch.

Sinners burning
in the pit,
twisting in a
tortured fit.

On the fringes,
those who smile,
winsome maids whom
fiends beguile.

Be wary then,
avoid all caves,
lest you become
my master's slaves.

The Witches' Bower

Leigh Blackmore

From winter's black season beneath the red moon
When tempests blow hard 'neath pale fretwork of stars,
When the surly gods seem to be crying a croon
Like frogs croaking loudly and lonely nightjars,

The season is changing to bountiful spring.
The hearts of the witches are filled with delight
As all dance in joy in their small faery ring,
And luminous boles glow in silent sunlight.

The softness and sweetness of fruit on the bough,
Made piquant with roses that bring the lovethirst,
Combine to make witches wear garlands at brow
And honour the Maid Mother winter has nursed.

Now here in the bower, their veins beat with song
As athames, censers, and candles adorn
The high sacred altar, the spring to prolong
With chalices, ruby wine, wands, and oaths sworn.

These nymphs and these satyrs who love the old Craft
And languidly cling in the bower's embrace
Call the Charge of the Goddess aloud; their witchcraft
Is truly the craft of the Wise, and of grace.

As petals drop quiet to make a soft bed,
The witches entwine in their love-rite so fair.
The altar with pentacle, wand, and cornbread
Bears witness so silent to each witch's prayer.

And as golden evening descends on the flower
Of youthful and Crone-like together this night,
The witches raise energy, send Cones of Power
To alter the world from its wrongness to right.

Warnings to the Curious

Frank Coffman

"The hotel room was adequate, pleasant enough.
Weary as I was, any haven would suffice.
Without, the wind howled wildly, cold as ice.
A sleet- and hail-filled time, the journey rough
From Salem out to Arkham in my car.
But I could barely see the road before me!
I can't recall a night so fierce and stormy;
It took three grueling hours, though not that far.

"Upon the nightstand, close beside the bed,
There lay a book—'A Bible,' I thought at first—
'But this one's odd?' Not covered black or red
Like most of them. And it was in the worst
Condition I had ever seen. Its pages
Were dark-discolored and its cover worn:
A dingy yellow—a most sickly hue!
Strangely, I felt uneasy just to view
The thing. And, stranger still, no words were borne
Upon the cover. So, I looked inside.

"I should have stopped when I read that old scrawl
Upon the flyleaf's formerly blank face:
'By all that's holy, don't read beyond this place!
Friend, if you value your sanity and all
Or any joys you've known ere reading this,
Put this tome down or thrown it in the fire!—

Destroy it! Though that is my great desire,
Having read—I can't—and now there is no bliss,
No comfort for me now, no going back
To the life I had before I read this book.
For that old, normal world I have forsook,
Now I am doomed—and all my vistas black!'

"Somehow, despite this weird and warning note,
I felt myself compelled to turn the leaf
To see if that was all the scribbler wrote—
Then saw the title page. This tome of grief
Was one I'd heard of many years ago.
'The stuff of legend,' I had always thought,
'A myth to frighten.' So I'd never sought
To find it, let alone to seek to know
What lay within those pages steeped in lore.
But now I held a copy in my hands.
I thought, 'What harm to just explore
The first few pages?'
                      "No one understands
The pull that awful book has on one's mind
Until they have the misfortune, as I did,
To read those horrid words that should be hid
In the darkest depths of Hell that one could find!

***

"So, stranger, heed you well these words of warning:
Reading *The King in Yellow* dooms your soul!
Your life becomes a night that knows no morning,
No solace as your few scant seasons roll
On toward those horrors that words cannot define.
For I have seen the King in yellow tatters,
Carcosa, and the realms where reason shatters,
The Old Ones terrible, The Yellow Sign!

"What of my mind remains tells me I should
Destroy this book—in the name of all that's good
And holy. And I'd destroy it—if I could!
I leave that task to you. Do not read on!
Resist that urge. And learn to love the dawn!"

* * *

"*How curious,*" he thought, "*clearly two different hands?*"
The book in his hotel room's bedside drawer
Was one that he had heard of oft before.
'*By all that's holy . . .*' and '*No one understands . . .*'
    He'd been hired as Miskatonic's latest sage.
    "*What harm?*" he thought . . .
                                    then turned another page.

Winter

Ian Futter

Winter arrives in a frost-coated coffin
carried by corpses, hail-hacked as they pass.
Ice husks, they trudge on hard ground that won't soften,
bearing their load through the months of cold glass.

Animals sleep and the birds cease their singing.
Lamps light and fires blaze to burn out the dark.
Spiders of snow drift through air that is stinging.
Fingers of frost lift the lid of dead bark.

Whining north winds mourn the passing of summer.
Skeleton trees rattle branches and moan.
Winter awakes, greets the funeral drummer
and slides through the world turning beauty to bone.

Chronoscape Advisory

Manuel Pérez-Campos

The only bewitchment is to have existed:
It is in the heat of the past that the great
mirages of history burn. There by scrying
have I daydreamed the Rhodes Colossus, sojourned
in Alexandria at its apogee,
and soared through miasma-smitten boroughs
laid waste by the Black Death. There are those who raise
towers from which to throw themselves into what
is yet to be. They never arrive. It is
not that nothingness out of which earth allots
you into the present at every moment,
gyring improbably, that is your home, but
the past, that groundedness away from you in
time you are being grafted into, making
you a stranger to yourself: It is there that you
live always, possessed of mythical vigor.

Lazarus Laments

Allan Rozinski

Believing the long trial of
suffering had ended,
released at last to the
mercy of final rest,
delivered unto
that blessed darkness
that knows no birth or death . . .
until he was rudely roused,
born again
into the tumult and noise,
the dirt and squalor, the scabrous filth
of the world he'd left behind;
where monsters and crueler gods do dwell
to feed humanity a steady diet of hell,
as he further awakened
to the horrific realization
that there may yet be even
worse things to come . . .
Was this the beginning
of a boundless chain
of unwanted lives to live,
an endless refrain
of nightmare worlds
that lie beyond this one?

Classic Reprints

The Deserted House

Lizette Woodworth Reese

The old house stands deserted, gray,
    With sharpened gables high in air,
And deep-set lattices, all gay
    With massive arch and framework rare;
And o'er it is a silence laid,
That feeling, one grows sore afraid.

The eaves are dark with heavy vines;
    The steep roof wears a coat of moss;
The walls are touched with dim designs
    Of shadows moving slow across;
The balconies are damp with weeds,
Lifting as close as streamside reeds.

The garden is a loved retreat
    Of melancholy flowers, of lone
And wild-mouthed herbs, in companies sweet,
    'Mid desolate green grasses thrown;
And in its gaps the hoar stone wall
Lets sprays of tangled ivy fall.

The pebbled paths drag, here and there,
    Old lichened faces, overspun
With silver spider-threads—they wear
    A silence sad to look upon:

It is so long since happy feet
Made them to thrill with pressure sweet.

'Mid drear but fragrant shrubs there stands
        A saint of old made mute in stone,
With tender eyes and yearning hands,
        And mouth formed in a sorrow lone;
'T is thick with dust, as long ago
'T was thick with fairest blooms that grow.

Swallows are whirring here and there;
        And oft a little soft wind blows
A hundred odors down the air;
        The bees hum 'round the red, last rose;
And ceaselessly the crickets shrill
Their tunes, and yet, it seems so still.

Or else, from out the distance steals,
        Half heard, the tramp of horses, or
The bleak and harsh stir of slow wheels
        Bound cityward; but more and more,
As these are hushed, or yet increase,
About the old house clings its peace.

[From Reese's *A Handful of Lavender* (Boston: Houghton, Mifflin, 1893).]

The Dark House

Edwin Arlington Robinson

Where a faint light shines alone,
Dwells a Demon I have known.
Most of you had better say
"The Dark House," and go your way.
Do not wonder if I stay.

For I know the Demon's eyes,
And their lure that never dies.
Banish all your fond alarms,
For I know the foiling charms
Of her eyes and of her arms,

And I know that in one room
Burns a lamp as in a tomb;
And I see the shadow glide,
Back and forth, of one denied
Power to find himself outside.

There he is who is my friend,
Damned, he fancies, to the end—
Vanquished, ever since a door
Closed, he thought, for evermore
On the life that was before.

And the friend who knows him best
Sees him as he sees the rest

Who are striving to be wise
While a Demon's arms and eyes
Hold them as a web would flies.

All the words of all the world,
Aimed together and then hurled,
Would be stiller in his ears
Than a closing of still shears
On a thread made out of years.

But there lives another sound,
More compelling, more profound;
There's a music, so it seems,
That assuages and redeems,
More than reason, more than dreams.

There's a music yet unheard
By the creature of the word,
Though it matters little more
Than a wave-wash on a shore—
Till a Demon shuts a door.

So, if he be very still
With his Demon, and one will,
Murmurs of it may be blown
To my friend who is alone
In a room that I have known.

After that from everywhere
Singing life will find him there;
Then the door will open wide,
And my friend, again outside,
Will be living, having died.

[From Robinson's *The Man against the Sky* (New York: Macmillan, 1916).]

Articles

Clark Ashton Smith and Robert Nelson: Master and Apprentice (Part 2)

Marcos Legaria

> In the visions that became apparent to me preceding and during the
> composition of *Dream-Stair* I had actually seen the goats *weeping*.
> —Robert Nelson to Clark Ashton Smith, 3 April 1934[1]

Following Farnsworth Wright's acceptance of "Sable Revery,"[2] Robert
Nelson hesitatingly unveiled the good news to his parents, Elmer (1884–
1978) and Ella Nelson (1889–1974). Robert was an only child. Both
parents, who were born in Sweden, installed themselves permanently by
1930 at 1030 Elm St., St. Charles, Illinois. Of his parents' attitude
toward him, Nelson wrote:

> I read your letter aloud to my parents, and, I am happy to say, it
> changed their attitude somewhat. However, they are still insisting that I
> secure immediate employment, and this I am doing my utmost to do.
>
> This coming summer I may not be able to make a tour of the West and
> meet and visit you at Auburn, but I surely hope to do so the next summer. I

---

1. Nelson, letter to Smith (3 April 1934); ms., John Hay Library, Brown
University (hereafter JHL).
2. "Sable Revery," *Weird Tales* 24, No. 3 (September 1934).

see now your own situation. And even though it may not be entirely free from care and worry it nevertheless is most noble and something to admire.[3]

At the time Smith was caring for his ailing parents, so a meeting of master and apprentice would not be convenient. But Nelson could make a second visit to Farnsworth Wright at the office of *Weird Tales* in Chicago. Nelson writes to Smith on 13 March 1934:

> He asked me again in this second interview if I was eighteen. I am taken by many for being even younger. I am nearly 22, as I have inferred [sic] before. I have wavy brown–blonde hair and dark brown eyes. It was only a few years ago that my hair was of a golden blonde color. But since then it has steadily been turning darker until, I fear, that a few years hence it will be entirely black.[4]

Nelson's thoughts of what kind of weird fiction should be and should not be in *Weird Tales*, as imparted to Smith, provide some snapshots of a young man very mature for his age:

> Secretly, Mr. Smith, I had often thought of reading some of the poems in W.T., [. . .] if I couldn't do any better than *that!* So, as you have seen, I have endeavored to compose a poem that is not only a poem, but also a weird poem, the sort of poem that should be in Weird Tales. [. . .]
>
> Most of us have grown tired of vampires, werewolves, and witches, and other weird senilities. This is 1934 and we demand new terrors.[5]

This philosophy of Nelson's would be reflected in the May 1934 issue of the *Fantasy Fan*, in his aptly titled "The Weird Tale (A Dialogue)." Concerning the sketch, Nelson wrote: "I think it is a little classic. The only thing, Hornig insisted on a cheap ending."[6] In between his letter to Smith and the *Fantasy Fan* appearance of his dialogue, Nelson wrote to the "Your Views" department of the magazine's April 1934 issue, elaborating his conception of the horror story:

---

3. Nelson, letter to Smith (8 March 1934); ms., JHL.

4. Ibid.

5. Nelson, letter to Smith (13 March 1934); ms., JHL.

6. Nelson, letter to Smith (24 April 1934); ms., JHL. Nelson refers to Charles D. Hornig, editor of the *Fantasy Fan*.

In the horror story, one can find true beauty—beauty that is glorified from tossing seas of blackness—shining beauty that comes with cosmic fear, lurid silence, frightful death—all this and more fascinates one's apprehension of true art. "When people read these and say that they are distasteful to the well and normal mind" then these certain people should not read them. No one is compelling them to do such. And why do we wish to read a sinister tale of evil or monstrosities? Listen, readers! Those of us who know life and have grown tired of its futile strivings, its worries, its hard realities (and most of us have by now), are able to forget it all by steeping ourselves with the nameless terrors and evil spawns of that "darkness visible".

Quite a startling set of impressions from a precocious young adult only twenty-one years of age. Evidence of Nelson's views of the weird tale gradually transformed into two poems. Composition of "Dream-Stair" began in February 1934. "Under the Tomb" was begun in early March of that year.[7] The poems transcend in both content and imagery what Wright was publishing at the time in *Weird Tales*. By 19 March, Nelson was ready to send the poems to Smith for perusal:

I hope they won't prove altogether disappointing. In both of the poems, as they now stand, I do not believe you will find anything at all harsh or vague. And I have tried not to stumble in meter. If I shall ever be able to "land" these two present poems in W.T. I may write one or two more.[8]

Some note should be made of Nelson's work ethic, moods, and the relationship he had with his parents, factors that would contribute to his demise. The Great Depression was at its height, and time seemed to be running out for Nelson. His father worked as a mechanic at the Burgess-Norton manufacturing plant in Geneva, Illinois, a mile from his home on Elm Street, and strides painfully made by Nelson resulted in a position at the Murphy Shell Oil station on South Fifth Avenue. Nelson tells Smith of his progress on 19 March 1934:

7. Nelson, letter to Smith (8 March 1934); ms., JHL.
8. Nelson, letter to Smith (19 March 1934); ms., JHL.

I now have some seemingly good 'prospects' for employment, but *these* prospects are more often like inflated balloons which can and most always become punctured in the highly indefinite future. However, I still have hope. But if I do not secure any employment by this coming July 23 I fear something dreadful will happen to myself.[9]

It can be seen that Nelson is already hinting of suicide to Smith. The date of 23 July points to Nelson's birthday; he would die the following year on the eve of this date. Darkening signs of his character are delineated in the closing paragraph from his letter of 19 March, focusing "Dream-Stair" and "Under the Tomb": "At the beginning of this letter I thought highly of my poems, but as I look upon them again I feel disgusted with both the poems and myself. Let me know what you think of the poems. I'll gladly welcome either praise or condemnation."[10]

A week later, Nelson was still lamenting the state of his recent poems: "I hope my newest poems do not prove too disappointing. And I hope I am not wasting any of your time. You are the *only* person, Mr. Smith, who has given me any *real* encouragement. And this I shall never forget as long as I live."[11]

The situation in Nelson's life at home wasn't looking any better, as he confided to Smith on 29 March:

Living with my parents is becoming more and more unbearable. It is very possible that in a month or two from now I shall be leaving my home and parents for ever. I have in mind to rent a quiet room or garret in Chicago. I still have in possession some of the money of my recently *matured* insurance policy. And this should last me for a time. I am positive that ultimately I shall be able to secure permanent employment of some sort, something that would at least pay my living expenses and give me time to write. If not, I dread to think what will happen.[12]

---

9. Nelson, letter to Smith (19 March 1934); ms., JHL.

10. Ibid.

11. Nelson, letter to Smith (29 March 1934); ms., JHL.

12. Ibid.

Nelson temporarily achieved some job security, but his relationship with his parents remained turbulent. His opposition to capitalism emerges from this turmoil, as he tells Smith on 3 April:

> I am both happy and sad tonight. I just secured employment. But it is only temporary, and is scheduled to last until the middle part of May or the first part of June. But even so, it has changed entirely the whole aspect of my parents' attitude towards me. Anything in which to 'make money' is their idea! In truth, all those who seek for riches and personal gain are, at better, both low in intellect and morals. The *highest* man of finance and business are the *lowest* in true intellect and good morals.
>
> As I have said before, I have never understood (and admired) my parents, and likewise they have never understood (and admired) me. Most parents possess that complete lack of logical and human understanding of their children, to the sense that they (the children) are their 'own flesh and blood,' and can, therefore, be molded into the sort of beings that they (the parents) 'intend to have *all* the right to expect.' All of which, of course, is plain unmitigated blah.
>
> Parents always judge and adjudicate their children. But there is a time when children should be the judges of their parents. And I, surely, have reached the age when I can assume the role of judicator. If I were to marry a girl on the morrow, should I ask my parents for consent or even the parents of my fiancée for their approval? Why should I? The parents have nothing to do with our love affair at all. If the two of us are agreed, there would be no occasion for a third party to assist us in our concord.[13]

The exact source of the friction between Nelson and his parents may never be known.

Nelson's appreciation of Smith's work can be discerned from the same letter about his parents. Praise of Smith's *The Double Shadow and Other Fantasies* has been noted, but now a fuller account not just of Smith's fiction but also his artwork, as Nelson conveyed it to Smith, sheds some light as to his varied tastes:

> I enjoyed your *The Death of Malygris* in the new April issue of Weird Tales even more so than The Charnel God. The illustration accompanying

---

13. Nelson, letter to Smith (3 April 1934); ms., JHL.

the former seems to me to be the best you have had so far. This decidedly weird drawing should evoke some comment of praise in the Eyrie.

There always tends to be a bit of grim humor interwoven, at times, in all your stories. And this is most enjoyable. For instance, in *The Death of Malygris*, when Nygon murmurs, "Behold, it is only the lich of an oldman [sic] after all, and one that has cheated the worm of his due provender over long." And in *The Charnel God*, when Pharion "glared with implacable suspicion at Abnon-Tha," and said, "Elaith was not dead, but only as one in trance,"—this after Abnon-Tha had exclaimed "she awoke ere the incantation was finished!"[14]

Nelson's praise of Smith's work—notably his poetry—was noted by Farnsworth Wright to Clark Ashton Smith on 1 March 1934: "It was Nelson who told me of the inclusion of three of your poems in the anthology compiled by Wallace Alvin Briggs."[15] Nelson's exact remarks to Wright survive in the following letter to Smith dated 3 April 1934:

> The other Saturday afternoon while browsing in a bookstore I came across a volume entitled, *Great Poems of the English Language* compiled by Wallace Alvin Briggs, (Tudor Pub. Co., New York.) Glancing on the outside cover-jacket I noted: 'Dr. Briggs has spent more than twenty years in the construction of this work, selecting representative poems from each of the great versifiers in our language from Chaucer down to the moderns.' Then fancy my mingled surprise and jubilation when I saw three of your poems in this great book of immortals.[16]

By this time Nelson was making poetic strides, and his philosophy of what a true weird poem evolved in his conceptions of "Under the Tomb" and "Dream-Stair":

> I can see that the composition of poetry, which has distinction as its aim, is much slower and more difficult than the writing of most prose. For example, when I look upon my *Under the Tomb*, I hear a voice screaming in

---

14. Nelson, letter to Smith (29 March 1934); ms., JHL.

15. Wright, letter to Smith (1 March 1934); ms., JHL.

16. Nelson, letter to Smith (3 April 1934); ms., JHL. The three poems by Smith included by Briggs are "Impression," "Recompense," and "Transcendence."

my ear "Fool! You are no poet!" And this poem, as you read it, is vague and unappealing. I admit. But thanks again for your otherwise hopeful encouragement.

I do not know why I even attempted *Under the Tomb*. I can say that I had imagined a vision of being under the hill. However, I do not believe that I had really *experienced* the vision in that utter 'reality' of dreams, from which I gathered *Dream-Stair*. When I say in *Under the Tomb* "Ah, but had he lived he would have writ, etc." I believe I had unknowingly taken the dead poet's place, endeavoring to remedy his position on earth had he lived! Yet, at the same time, I had also tried to accompany him while *in* the tomb and far beneath, (which could only be seen while in the *tomb*)! But I shall leave the poem rest for awhile and then attempt to rewrite it.[17]

Visions and voices found inspiration in "Under the Tomb," but dreams and reality blur and become interchangeable in "Dream-Stair":

In the visions that became apparent to me preceding and during the composition of *Dream-Stair* I had actually seen the goats weeping. Also, I had seen *myself* down in the halls below among them, not only weeping with them myself, but also kissing and nuzzling them between sobs! This may seem extravagantly fantastic but it is the truth. You must forgive me if the knowledge of my dreams prove distasteful to you. I have had others more fantastic, more ludicrous, more horrible. But I can see, perhaps, that in the *poem* "weeping goats" sounds, as say, a bit ludicrous. But a goat really does have a sad and kind face, if you look closely at one.[18]

Nelson outlines some of the original lines in the poem, as well as Smith's revisions: "Your lines, 'that grasps and throttles all the Gorgon's asps. And dares the Gorgon's eyes to slay,' is quite novel and powerful."[19] He indicates what he had originally written before Smith's revision of the lines: "I was wondering what you thought of my lines, 'With poisoned florid hands, that reach and choke asps gorged, and beseech blight-beautiful women to slay.'"[20] In the long run, Nelson believed this

---

17. Ibid.
18. Ibid.
19. Ibid.
20. Ibid.

might be a bit much for Smith, so the matter of additional revisions for "Dream-Stair" was put on hold: "From now on I hope to be more moderate and more painstaking in the labor of my literary compositions."[21] Nelson had high hopes submitting "Dream-Stair" to Wright sometime in early May.[22]

Doubts began to creep in about some of Smith's lines incorporated in "Dream-Stair," as he shared his feelings with Smith in his postcard of 25 April 1934:

> As I said, I thought the suggestion of the G.[23] and the *asps* 'quite novel and powerful.' But I have gone over and over the whole thing and I now think it is a bit *too* powerful and *tends* somewhat toward the ludicrous. Then, too, I don't care for my own lines either. But I shall put forth both versions to W. And will let you know of course, the outcome.[24]

Nelson meant no disrespect for Smith's suggested revisions; he merely wished to point out a commonplace trope in weird fiction that he detested: "Perhaps my own hatred towards the boorish waving of crosses before vampires has somewhat influenced my dislike of Medusa-headed nightmares!"[25]

By early May 1934, Nelson had met with Wright a third time at the *Weird Tales* office and personally delivered the revised "Dream-Stair." Before acceptance, Wright requested that Nelson trim the poem down from its original 44 lines to 36 lines, as it was too long for the page.[26] Nelson's earlier doubts about some of Smith's lines were unfounded: "Many, many thanks again for the Gorgon suggestions. Pay no attention to some of my *ideas!* They change often and many times."[27] Of the two

---

21. Ibid.

22. Nelson, letter to Smith (24 April 1934); ms., JHL.

23. The G. stands for Gorgon.

24. Nelson, postcard to Smith (postmarked 25 April 1934); ms., JHL.

25. Ibid.

26. Nelson, postcard to Smith (postmarked 7 May 1934); ms., JHL.

27. Nelson, letter to Smith (11 May 1934); ms., JHL.

poems, Nelson confided to Smith that he still preferred "Sable Revery" over "Dream-Stair," as it was "of a finer quality."[28]

Around mid-May 1934, Nelson told Smith that Wright finally accepted "Dream-Stair." This postcard to Smith is priceless, as Nelson details some of the lines that were deleted within "Dream-Stair": "The eight lines that I sacrificed are, etc., and the first four beginning with 'Mask upon mask of horror now, etc.' This I thought, was the best I could do, without wholly impairing the color of imagery."[29]

Perusal of "Dream-Stair," with Smith's revisions and freshly edited as published in its final form in the April 1935 issue of *Weird Tales*, is warranted:

> What naked, bald and drunken child
> Leads me to some mad, topless stair
> And keeps me toiling upward there,
> A withered thing, forlorn and wild?
> About me swarm Satanic goats,
> The seas below are frothing red,
> And harsh winds sting my seething head
> As steel on stone drops down in moats
> Where drown and rot accursèd swains—
> Dismembered thralls of some mad king—
> Whose bloating heads arise and sing.
> But, lo! whence all these hellish rains
> That seem to linger for an age
> And pour upon my harried life
> Such airs, with loathsome larvæ rife,
> As whisper o'er a wizard's page?
> Then, mounting with white moons, I see
> The frenzied flight of huge man-birds,
> And hear the cold and lethal words
> Babbled behind that drapery
> Whose swelling folds lean forth and sway,
> Shrouding a handed Shape, that grasps

---

28. Ibid.

29. Nelson, postcard to Smith (15 May 1934); ms., JHL.

And throttles all the Gorgon's asps,
And braves the Gorgon's eyes to slay!
The child brings ardent wine to me,
And still I climb the dream-built stair;
And in fell silence spreading there
Great shadows eat the spherèd sea.
False child! false child! O traitor child!
What Image meets my frozen eyes?
Is It what Satan sanctifies—
Full-fraught with bale but pleasing mild?
But the stair crumbles, clean destroyed,
The circling mists and phantoms flee,
The child pursues them mad with glee,
And leaves me in the falling void.

This wouldn't be the last word on "Dream-Stair." The eight deleted lines that did not make the final cut soon found their way into Nelson's latest creation, as he notified Smith:

> I am enclosing a new poem of mine, entitled, "Jorgas."[30] I have employed in part, almost all of the substance of the excised lines of "Dream-Stair." Most of the lines are iambic, some trochee. [. . .] And I do not know what to think of "Jorgas." However, let me know whether I should consign it to the flames or not.[31]

Nelson felt the same way about "Under the Tomb." In its earlier incarnation, even Smith found it "vague and unappealing."[32] Nelson wrote to Smith on 24 April 1934: "Perhaps instead of burning 'Under the Tomb,' I shall save and employ it in some future fantasy for Fantasy Fan, which would really be the same as burning it anyway."[33]

---

30. "Jorgas," *Weird Tales* 27, No. 2 (February 1936): 187.

31. Nelson, letter to Smith (28 May 1934); ms., JHL.

32. Nelson, letter to Smith (3 April 1934); ms., JHL.

33. Nelson, letter to Smith (24 April 1934); ms., JHL.

Reviews

Witches, Traditional and Otherwise

Leigh Blackmore

ASHLEY DIOSES, ed. *Eye to the Telescope.* No. 30 (October 2018): "Witches." Science Fiction Poetry Association. eyetothetelescope.com/archives/030issue.html

The witch figure has, literarily and historically, often been scorned, disdained, and even feared. Dioses explains in her introduction to this themed issue that she deliberately left the definition of witch broad, allowing it to range from cunning women or healers to seers and oracles.

The issue presents sixteen poems from as many different poets. Alexandra Seidel's "Seven Witches" is a long freeform piece in which six of seven witches who ride out to the sun have different needs, leading them to leave the group; at last but one witch still rides. K. A. Opperman's "The Crimson Witch," an octet in couplets, effectively portrays the traditional *femme fatale* witch-image. William Cook's "Commemoration of the Divine Passion," in eleven long unrhymed stanzas, evokes a witch-burning with nature imagery (most of which works acceptably well, save the phrase "black amphibious wine"), and a bereft lover's search. Joseph Maddrey riffs on both Thomas De Quincey and on Dario Argento's 'Three Mothers' witchcraft film trilogy in "Our Ladies of Sorrow." Dan Clore deftly portrays the essential witchcraft practice of conjuring the elemental powers in "Dream Sonnet for Ashiel."

Adam Bolivar continues his use of folklore in "Jack and the Hex Witch" as a traditional wily witch attempts, but fails, to seduce Jack. In "Masque," a miniature epic by F. J. Bergmann, the poet delights in antique language relating the fate of a man who attends an All Hallow's Eve ball, and the woman who allures him there. "The Ladies of Lancashire" are in fact lights suspended from a 'witching tree' in Clay F. Johnson's poem; they destroy a party of churchmen. Lucy Ann Fiorini's "Circe," though following the pattern of witches whose magic 'makes men die,' has an effective circular closure, returning to its opening line. The demonization of the witch is seen again in Zoey Xolton's "The Devil's Mistress," but one cannot deny the poem's effectiveness within its ideological limits.

By contrast, Ann Schwader's "Two Meetings" is a strong feminist take on the wise witch and her craft, and a condemnation of the fearful patriarchy which in darker times caused daughters and wives to be condemned as instruments of the Devil. "To Make Our World Bleed" is another effective 'traditional' portrayal of the dark witch, as Adam Wassil's "Beware the Dance of the Witches for with It They Serve Apollyon" seems to be. "Aisha's Revenge" by D. L. Myers, well-written but over-familiar in theme, turns on the fate meted out by a burned witch's curse. Jessica Amanda Salmonson's short "Wild Aseneth" walks a fine path between depicting the hag as actually evil or as mere omen. All in all, a fine mixture of verse in both free and rhymed form.

A Poetic Original

Donald Sidney-Fryer

G. SUTTON BREIDING. *Ill Desperado, 2013/2014.* A collection of ten free-verse and/or free form poems. A booklet 8½ × 11 inches, 12 pages, glossy black cover (some kind of card material), poems photocopied from elegantly hand printed sheets. An edition de luxe as a privately printed or published book or booklet. Issued only to friends and fellow poets. August 2018.

In its own way *Ill Desperado*—the title is a clever take on Gérard de Nerval's melancholic sonnet "El Desdichado"—is almost as exceptional (although much smaller and with different proportions) as Frank Coffman's tome *The Coven's Handbook* (2018/2019).

On the dedication page of his *Selected Poems*, Clark Ashton Smith quotes what seems his own translation of the first four lines of Nerval's lyrical poem "El Desdichado." Nerval is that unique precursor as a great poet to Baudelaire with *Les Fleurs du mal,* just as Aloysius Bertrand with his *Gaspard de la Nuit* is the unique precursor to Baudelaire with his *Poèmes en prose.*

> I am that dark, that disinherited,
> That all-dishonored prince of Aquitaine.
> The star upon my scutcheon long hath fled,
> A black sun on my lute doth yet remain.

This translation might also be from the pen of Arthur Symons. Whether in English or in French, it has very strong affinities with the final poem in Sutton Breiding's most recent collection. We quote this final poem in full to demonstrate him as a full-fledged legatee of Nerval, Baudelaire, and Rimbaud, albeit an original and considerable figure in his own right, and one who mines his own vein of melancholy and the beautiful, no less his disaffection or discontent with his own era.

> I am that wasted
> that dysfunctional troubadour
> hanging in a noose of silk stockings
> from the overburdened lamp post of hopes
> above the Stygian gutters
> where my diamond sonnets putrefy
> I snap my lute strings one by one
> disconsolate as a neutron sun
> in the toxic void of that birth canal where Death was waiting
> with the charred escutcheon of my inheritance
> smeared all over in the blackest of lipsticks
> of all the kisses I dishonored with a poem

I have long followed the life and career of Sutton Breiding, probably since the later 1960s in San Francisco, where I lived during 1965–75, in fact through the whole hippie period. We most likely met through the auspices of Don Herron, himself a recent arrival from Tennessee, just as Sutton and his family, mother and siblings, hailed from Morgantown, West Virginia. They resided at that time in a several-storied family house in the Haight-Ashbury district. I myself resided in a big flat in a similar but larger building not far from where Haight and Ashbury intersect.

Soon Sutton began issuing the notable series of his handmade and homemade booklets containing his poetry, at once free verse and free form, remarkable for its depth and the great variety of its wide-ranging imagery. We often visited back and forth between our respective domiciles, and I even stayed overnight at the Breiding abode several times, in addition to sharing their regular meals. They made a lively and enjoyable household. We passed many pleasant evenings together, and I cherish the memories that I still have of those happy times.

Of course, we had all become united through our fervid interest in modern imaginative literature as purveyed not only by Lovecraft, Smith, Robert E. Howard, etc., but also by *Weird Tales* and Arkham House, i.e., August Derleth. And here we wish to pay tribute, a big tribute, to a veteran and fellow poet, one G. Sutton Breiding, on the basis of his last booklet, in case we have not so done before.

Sutton has assuredly stayed the course, whether receiving laudation or brickbats. He has followed his own star, his own Muse, forthrightly. That says a lot for a poet in America who does not receive mainstream recognition. At his age Sutton should have a volume of his collected poems published in his honor by some acolyte in conjunction with a small press other than the poet's own. Let us quote some random lines from his latest booklet to give the reader an idea of Sutton's range and characteristic imagery. Let us grant the poet himself the last significant word or phrase.

chewing on air
I chase my manias in shrinking circles
hypnotized by the psychedelic monitors
in the hospital of words

it's the tragedy of the mystic impulse
bejeweled staircases going nowhere
magical toys that broke long ago

I medicate
with words and walks
gaze at the river in supernatural dawns

what is all this starry-eyed nonsense
the smeared snot of dreams all over the place

I ride my skeleton horse to Death
the beggar king of fog and off ramps
out among the powerlines and derelict toilets

the past was once a Goth chanteuse
crooning in the dead city of my heart

I am haunted unto madness
by the strangeness of this world

from the slimy troughs of verse

I dig my way to another unrequited day

I croak and stutter over stacks of paper
my hands hardening into the luminous mud of language

I'm on my way there down that dark lane
with my solid gold jetpack strapped on tightly

in the meantime my rotting head
screams out its erotic dirges

and terminally ill chimaeras lick at me
with the barbed and merciless piercings
of their long and golden tongues

No doubt about it, G. Sutton Breiding remains one of the poetic
originals of our time and still abides with us!

Notes on Contributors

By day, **Mike Allen** writes the arts column for the *Roanoke* (VA) *Times*. By night he spins dark fables. An author, editor, and publisher, he has been a finalist for the Nebula, Shirley Jackson, and World Fantasy Awards, as well as a three-time winner of the Rhysling Award for poetry.

Manuel Arenas is what Howard Phillips Lovecraft would have called an "epicure of the terrible." He resides on Phoenix, Arizona, where he pens his Gothic fantasies and dark ditties sheltered behind heavy curtains, as he shuns the oppressive orb which glares down on him from the cloudless, dust-filled desert sky.

Ross Balcom lives in Southern California. His poems have appeared in *Beyond Centauri, inkscrawl, Poetry Midwest, Scifaikuest, Star*Line*, and other publications. He is a frequent contributor to *Songs of Eretz Poetry Review*.

David Barker has published two collections of short horror fiction written in collaboration with W. H. Pugmire: *The Revenant of Rebecca Pascal* (2014) and *In the Gulfs of Dream and Other Lovecraftian Tales* (2015). Their Lovecraftian novel, *Witches in Dreamland*, was published by Hippocampus Press in 2018.

Barbara Barrett is an author and a published poet who loves and appreciates words. Her articles have appeared on blogs, websites, and in fanzines. Several of her essays have received awards from the Robert E. Howard Foundation. She lives in California, where she is currently compiling a book of her fiction and poetry.

F. J. Bergmann edits poetry for *Mobius: The Journal of Social Change* and imagines tragedies on or near exoplanets. His work appears irregularly in *Analog, Asimov's, Polu Texni, Pulp Literature, Silver Blade*, and elsewhere. A *Catalogue of the Further Suns*, a collection of dystopian first-contact poems, won the 2017 Gold Line Press poetry chapbook contest and is available at fibitz.com.

Leigh Blackmore has written weird verse since age thirteen. He has lived in the Illawarra, New South Wales, Australia, for the last decade. He has edited *Terror Australis: Best Australian Horror* (1993) and *Midnight Echo 5* (2011) and written *Spores from Sharnoth & Other Madnesses* (2008). A nominee for SFPA's Rhysling Award (Best Long Poem), Leigh is also a four-time Ditmar Award nominee. He is currently assembling an edition of *The Selected Letters of Robert Bloch.*

Adam Bolivar, a native of Boston now residing in Portland, Oregon, published his weird fiction and poetry in the pages of *Nameless*, the *Lovecraft eZine*, *Spectral Realms*, and Chaosium's *Steampunk Cthulhu* and *Atomic Age Cthulhu* anthologies. His latest collection, *The Lay of Old Hex*, was published in 2017 by Hippocampus Press.

Rich Catalano resides in Pittsburgh, Pennsylvania, and has been writing formalist poetry from a young age. He draws his inspiration from the English Romantic School as well as from weird writers such as Clark Ashton Smith, George Sterling, and H. P. Lovecraft. His main interest of study is the Western grimoiric tradition of ceremonial magic.

Frank Coffman is a retired professor of college English, creative writing, and journalism and has dedicated his retirement to creative writing and scholarly research. He has published both speculative poetry and fiction in a variety of magazines and anthologies. His book of collected poems, *The Coven's Handbook and Other Poems*, was released in January 2019. He edited Robert E. Howard's *Selected Poems.*

Scott J. Couturier hails from the far frigid lands of Northern Michigan. A novelist, poet, rock-'n'-roll archivist, and editor, his work has recently appeared in such venues as *The Audient Void*, *Spectral Realms*, *Weirdbook*, and the anthology series *Test Patterns*. In 2017 he released *The Curse of Roc-Thalian*, the third volume in his ongoing dark fantasy series *The Magistricide.*

Margi Curtis (MCA) is a witch, writer, artist, healer and activist, living in Wollongong, New South Wales, Australia. Published in magazines and anthologies, in print and online, she is the author of four collections of poetry. Her poem "A Deathless Love" appeared in *Midnight Echo* No. 5 (AHWA, 2011).

Ashley Dioses is a writer of dark fiction and poetry from Southern California. Her fiction and poetry has appeared in *Weird Fiction Review, Spectral Realms, Xnoybis, Weirdbook, Gothic Blue Book*, and elsewhere. Her debut collection of dark traditional poetry, *Diary of a Sorceress*, was published in 2017 by Hippocampus Press.

Poems by **Kendall Evans** have appeared in *Weird Tales, Analog, Asimov's,* and other magazines. His stories have appeared in *Amazing, Weirdbook, Fantastic,* and elsewhere. His novel *The Rings of Ganymede*, a ring cycle in the tradition of Wagner's operas and Tolkien's *Lord of the Rings*, was published by Alban Lake Books in 2014.

Ian Futter began writing stories and poems in his childhood, but only lately has started to share them. One of his poems appears in *The Darke Phantastique* (Cycatrix Press, 2014), and he continues to produce dark fiction for admirers of the surreal.

Joshua Gage is an ornery curmudgeon from Cleveland. He is the author of five collections of poetry. His newest chapbook, *Necromancy,* is available on Locofo Chaps from Moria Press. He is a graduate of the Low Residency MFA Program in Creative Writing at Naropa University. He has a penchant for Pendleton shirts and any poem strong enough to yank the breath out of his lungs.

Liam Garriock is an author, prose-poet, and aspiring polymath who lives in Edinburgh, Scotland, or, alternatively, in a metaphysical borderland between "Aubrey Beardsley's ideally grotesque world" and Joseph Cornell's nostalgic dreamland. He likes to remain elusive.

Wade German is the author of *Dreams from a Black Nebula* (Hippocampus Press, 2014). His poetry has been nominated for the Pushcart, Rhysling, and Elgin Awards, and has received numerous honorable mentions in Ellen Datlow's *Best Horror of the Year* anthologies.

Jeff Hall is a software developer and graduate student living in Seattle. A lifelong fan of weird fiction, he only recently dove head-first into the poetry corpus of Clark Ashton Smith. That experience, combined with a re-reading of John Keats's poetic works, had a profound impact on him, resulting in his first published appearance in this issue of *Spectral Realms*.

Chad Hensley is a Bram Stoker Award–nominated author. His fiction and poetry have received honorable mentions in *The Year's Best Fantasy and Horror*. His most recent book of poetry, *Embrace the Hideous Immaculate*, was published by Raw Dog Screaming Press. Look for his fiction in *Weirdbook* and *Eldritch Tales*. His nonfiction has appeared in *Rue Morgue*, *Terrorizer*, *Spin*, *Hustler*, *Juxtapoz*, *Super7* (where he was a contributing editor), and *Weird Fiction Review*.

Randall D. Larson has been writing Lovecraftian and Bloch-ian fiction and nonfiction since the 1970s (*Eldritch Tales*, *The Arkham Sampler*, *Crypt of Cthulhu*, *Weird Worlds*, *Inhuman*, etc.) and has contributed to a number of books on weird fiction criticism. The bulk of his writing has been in the realm of film and film music commentary.

Marcos Legaria is a scholar on H. P. Lovecraft, R. H. Barlow, Clark Ashton Smith, and related writers. His articles have appeared in the *Lovecraft Annual* and elsewhere.

Charles Lovecraft is a resident of Sydney, Australia, where he studies English at Macquarie University. He started writing in 1972, inspired by George Orwell. He began writing in earnest in 1975, inspired momentously by H. P. Lovecraft. As publisher-editor, Charles began P'rea Press (www.preapress.com) in 2007 to publish weird and fantastic poetry, criticism, and bibliography, and to keep traditional poetry forms alive. He has edited more than thirty books.

Kurt Newton is a short story writer and novelist, but his first love is, and always will be, poetry. Over the last twenty years his poetry has appeared in a wide variety of magazines and anthologies including *Dreams and Nightmares*, *Star*Line*, *Mythic Delirium*, *Polu Texni*, *Hinnom Magazine*, *Corpse Roads*, and *The Book of Night*.

Charles D. O'Connor III is a weird poet living in Virginia Beach, Virginia. He has an extensive collection of rare fiction material and runs a

Facebook page dedicated to R. H. Barlow. "Life can be difficult," he says, "but weird fiction saved my life, and has been good to me. I'll always be good to it."

Manuel Pérez-Campos's poetry has appeared previously in *Spectral Realms* and *Weird Fiction Review*. A collection of his poetry in the key of the weird is in progress; so is a collection of ground-breaking essays on H. P. Lovecraft. He lives in Bayamón, Puerto Rico.

Carl E. Reed is currently employed as the showroom manager for a window, siding, and door company just outside Chicago. His poetry has been published in the *Iconoclast*; short stories in *Black Gate* and *newWitch* magazines.

S. Brackett Robertson lives near many bodies of water. Brackett's work has previously appeared in *Goblin Fruit, Mythic Delirium, Inkscrawl,* and *Stone Telling.* Brackett enjoys museums and math and occasionally tweets at sbrackettr.

Allan Rozinski is a writer of speculative fiction and poetry who has most recently had poetry either accepted or published in *HWA Poetry Showcase Volume V, Spectral Realms, Outposts of Beyond, Star*Line,* and *Weirdbook.* He can be found on Facebook and Twitter.

Ann K. Schwader lives and writes in Colorado. Her most recent collections are *Dark Energies* (P'rea Press, 2015) and *Twisted in Dream* (Hippocampus Press, 2011). Her *Wild Hunt of the Stars* (Sam's Dot, 2010) and *Dark Energies* were Bram Stoker Award finalists. In 2018, she received the Science Fiction & Fantasy Poetry Association's Grand Master award. She is also a two-time Rhysling Award winner (2010 and 2015) and was the Poet Laureate for NecronomiCon Providence 2015.

Claire Smith's work mainly explores other worlds: the mythological, fairy tale, the supernatural and more. Her poetry has appeared, most recently, in journals and anthologies including earlier issues of *Spectral Realms, Illumen, Eye to the Telescope,* and *Riddled with Arrows.* She holds an M.A. in English from the Open University. She lives in Gloucestershire,

UK, with her husband, the writer Oliver Smith, and their very spoiled Tonkinese cat.

Oliver Smith is an artist and writer from Cheltenham, Gloucestershire, UK. His poetry has appeared in *Dreams & Nightmares, Eye to the Telescope, Illumen, Mirror Dance, Rivet, Spectral Realms, Star*Line,* and *Weirdbook.* His collection of stories, *Stars Beneath the Ships,* was published by Ex Occidente Press in 2017, and many of his previously anthologized stories and poems are collected in *Basilisk Soup and Other Fantasies.* Oliver is currently studying for a Ph.D. in Creative Writing.

Christina Sng is the Bram Stoker and Elgin Award–winning author of *A Collection of Nightmares* and *Astropoetry.* Her work has appeared in numerous venues worldwide and garnered over 70 awards and nominations, including the 2018 Jane Reichhold International Prize, the 2016 Harold G. Henderson Award, and Honorable Mentions in *The Year's Best Fantasy and Horror* and *Best Horror of the Year.*

Donald Sidney-Fryer is the author of *Songs and Sonnets Atlantean* (Arkham House, 1971), *Emperor of Dreams: A Clark Ashton Smith Bibliography* (Donald M. Grant, 1978), *The Atlantis Fragments* (Hippocampus Press, 2009), and many other volumes. He has edited Smith's *Poems in Prose* (Arkham House, 1965) and written many books and articles on California poets. His autobiography *Hobgoblin Apollo* (2016) and two volumes of miscellany, *Aesthetics Ho!* (2017) and *West of Wherevermore* (2019) have been published by Hippocampus Press.

Thomas Tyrrell has a Ph.D. in English Literature from Cardiff University. He is a two-time winner of the Terry Hetherington poetry award, and his writing has appeared in *Picaroon, Amaryllis, Wales Arts Review, isacoustic, Lonesome October, The Road Less Travelled, Three Days from a Cauldron,* and *Words for the Wild.*

Mary Krawczak Wilson has written poetry, fiction, plays, articles, and essays. She was born in St. Paul, Minnesota, and moved to Seattle in 1991. Her most recent essay appeared in the *American Rationalist.*

Index to *Spectral Realms* 1–10

Conspectus of issues:

1 = Summer 2014
2 = Winter 2015
3 = Summer 2015
4 = Winter 2016
5 = Summer 2016

6 = Winter 2017
7 = Summer2017
8 = Winter 2018
9 = Summer 2018
10 = Winter 2019

I. Index of Contributors

McLaughlin, Mark 3.23, 88
Mariconda, Steven J. 4.134–37
Martin, Sean Elliot 2.80–82
Matheny, Rob 8.54–55
Medsker, Josh 6.40
Merrill, Stuart 1.97
Merritt, A. 3.119
Miller, Michael D. 9.32
Mundy, John J. 3.32–33, 86; 4.8–9,
    60–61; 4.95; 5.15, 63, 94; 6.12–
    13, 49–50, 97–99
Myers, D. L. 1.21, 66; 2.26–27, 70;
    3.24, 68, 146–47; 4.6; 5.34, 76;
    6.16–17, 86

Newton, Kurt 10.20–21, 87
Nolan, William F. 2.42; 4.31

O'Connor III, Charles D. 2.60,
    106; 5.43–45; 7.76–77; 9.56–57;
    10.13
O'Shaughnessy, Arthur 8.96–97
Opperman, K. A. 1.12–13, 42–43,
    85; 2.43, 87, 106; 3.8–9, 74–75,
    108–9; 4.41, 86, 98–100; 5.54–
    55; 6.19–22, 7.41; 8.57; 9.48

Parkhurst, Russ 9.123–26
Pérez-Campos, Manuel 6.37, 73;
    7.24, 25, 67; 8.26–27, 80–81;
    9.53, 75, 94; 10.22, 64, 102
Phillips, Fred 1.55; 2.32, 62, 89;
    3.35; 4.101; 5.93
Pugmire, W. H. 1.28–29, 84; 2.63;
    5.35–36; 6.9
Pulver, Joseph S., Sr. 5.12–14, 88

Rajala, J.-M. 6.139–44
Ramsey, Shawn 8.59
Reed, Carl E. 10.41
Reed, Nathaniel 5.11, 53, 89–91;
    6.47, 82; 7.43
Reese, Lizette Woodworth 10.107–9
Reinhart, John 8.48
Robertson, S. Brackett 10.54–55
Robinson, Edwin Arlington
    10.109–10

Rozinski, Allan 9.34–35; 10.61,
    103

Salmonson, Jessica Amanda 6.24–
    25; 7.15, 46, 82–84; 8.12, 77;
    9.60, 82–83
Saltus, Edgar 5.105–6
Saltus, Francis S. 2.119–21
Schembri, David 1.67, 83; 2.54–55;
    8.58
Schultz, David E. 4.110
Schwader, Ann K. 1.10, 44–45;
    2.20, 72; 3.82; 4.17, 71; 5.25;
    6.112; 7.10, 56–57, 75; 8.90;
    9.15; 10.28–29
Schweitzer, Darrell 1.50; 2.35, 73;
    3.25; 4.70, 74; 5.17; 6.41; 8.44;
    9.44
Shelley, Percy Bysshe 4.107–8
Shirley, John 2.40–41, 94; 4.18–20;
    5.20–23, 72; 6.7–8, 92–93, 113;
    7.7–9, 50–52, 90–92, 113–16;
    8.82; 9.16–17, 64–65
Shorter, Dora Sigerson 9.101–2
Sidney-Fryer, Donald 1.105–20;
    2.7–19; 4.126–33; 9.117–20,
    126–30; 10.127–30
Simon, Marge 1.26–27; 2.48–49;
    3.106–7
Smith, Claire 1.58–59; 2.30–31;
    4.37; 6.30–31, 56–57, 94–95;
    7.48–49; 8.40–41; 10.14–15, 60–
    61
Smith, Farah Rose 6.58
Smith, Oliver 1.74–75; 2.103–05;
    3.110–11; 4.21–23, 88–90; 5.47–
    49, 96–97; 6.84–85, 6.108–9;
    8.29, 74; 10.56–57
Sng, Christina 3.10–12, 38, 99;
    4.7, 36, 92–94; 5.66–69; 5.84–
    87; 6.33–35, 64, 89, 110–11;
    7.21, 60–61; 8.24–25, 70–71;
    86–87; 9.28–29, 70, 92–93;
    10.18–19, 71–74
Sterling, George 1.93–95
Strange, Daniel Kolbe 1.68

Sturner, Jason 3.76
Swinburne, Algernon Charles
   2.122-27

Tatiana 9.59, 86
Terry, Ronald 6.18, 51, 88; 7.22,
   54-55
Thomas, Jonathan 1.14-15; 2.28-
   29, 67; 3.16-18, 62-63, 89;
   4.80-83; 5.64-65
Thomas, Scott 4.14, 87
Tibbetts, John C. 2.38-39, 74
Tierney, Richard L. 1.11, 65; 5.37;
   6.23, 96; 7.23; 8.10-11
Tyrer, DJ 3.21; 67, 101
Tyrrell, Thomas 10.7, 79-83

Ward, Kyla Lee 1.60-64; 4.32-35;
   6.53
Webb, Don 3.37; 7.47; 8.37
Webb, M. F. 2.76-77; 3.7; 4.10-
   11, 58-59; 5.9, 10; 6.44; 7.14,
   58, 85; 8.17, 75; 9.18-19
White, Michelle Claire 6.74-75
Wildes, Abigail 8.9
Wilson, Mary Krawczak 3.22, 98;
   4.25, 102; 5.24, 62; 6.29, 62;
   7.37, 79; 8.36, 79; 9.38, 72;
   10.40
Withrow, Steven 4.63
Wright, Farnsworth 8.95
Wytovich, Stephanie M. 2.66, 107

Yeats, W. B. 4.109

II. Index of Titles

"Absinthia" (Opperman) 4.41
"Acrostic Sonnet in Memory of
   Providence, R.I., 8 August 1936"
   (Lovecraft) 9.37
"Ad'Naigon" (Gold) 7.44-45
"Admonishments for the
   Incautious" (Barker) 6.83
"Adverse Star, The" (Blackmore)
   4.26
"Aenid's Dream" (Sng) 7.21
"Afrasiab Down the Oxus"
   (Lovecraft) 1.78
"After the Cryptozoic" (Evans)
   10.45
"Agents of Dread" (Barker) 5.100-
   101
"Alastor" (German) 4.84
"Alchemist's Disease, The" (Reed)
   5.53
"Alchemy" (Futter) 4.96-97
"Alive" (Pulver) 5.88
"All Masks Are Mirrors" (Schwader)
   5.25
"All Will Taste Death" (Balcom)
   10.77
"Alone in the Desert" (Wilson) 3.98

"Always Look under the Bed"
   (McLaughlin) 3.23
"Amenophra" (Edkins) 7.97-100
"Among the Gargoyles" (Opperman)
   4.86
"Among the Ghouls" (Opperman)
   2.43
"And Only Then I Saw" (Lovecraft)
   4.29
"Angel's Pen, The" (O'Connor III)
   9.56-57
"Angels, The" (de Banville, tr.
   Merrill) 1.97
"Angels All Are Corpses in the Sky,
   The" (Opperman) 1.85
"Angry Gods" (Wilson) 5.24
"Angry in His Grave" (Schweitzer)
   9.44
"Angry Sun/Bloated Moon" (Smith)
   7.48
"Another Knife-Grey Day" (Kelly)
   2.46
"Antagonist" (Bergmann) 5.58
"Antarktos Sequence" (Pérez-
   Campos) 9.53
"Applem, The" (Smith) 2.30-31

·

www.ingramcontent.com/pod-product-compliance
Lightning Source LLC
Chambersburg PA
CBHW060801050426
42449CB00008B/1475